Adoption

Other Books of Related Interest:

Opposing Viewpoints Series

Abortion

The Family

Interracial America

Population

Teenage Pregnancy

Teenage Sexuality

Current Controversies Series

The Abortion Controversy

Gay Rights

Issues in Adoption

Teen Pregnancy and Parenting

At Issue Series

Do Children Have Rights?

The Ethics of Abortion

Gay and Lesbian Families

Gay Marriage

"Congress shall make no law . . . abridging the freedom of speech, or of the press."

First Amendment to the U.S. Constitution

The basic foundation of our democracy is the First Amendment guarantee of freedom of expression. The Opposing Viewpoints Series is dedicated to the concept of this basic freedom and the idea that it is more important to practice it than to enshrine it.

Adoption

Mary E. Williams, Book Editor

GREENHAVEN PRESS

An imprint of Thomson Gale, a part of The Thomson Corporation

THOMSON

GALE™

Detroit • New York • San Francisco • New Haven, Conn. • Waterville, Maine • London • Munich

THOMSON

✳ ™

GALE

Bonnie Szumski, *Publisher*
Helen Cothran, *Managing Editor*

© 2006 Thomson Gale, a part of The Thomson Corporation.

Thomson and Star Logo are trademarks and Gale and Greenhaven Press are registered trademarks used herein under license.

For more information, contact:
Greenhaven Press
27500 Drake Rd.
Farmington Hills, MI 48331-3535
Or you can visit our Internet site at http://www.gale.com

LIBRARY OF CONGRESS CATALOGING-IN-PUBLICATION DATA

Adoption / Mary E. Williams, book editor.
   p. cm. -- (Opposing viewpoints)
  Includes bibliographical references and index.
  0-7377-3302-0 (pbk.)   0-7377-3301-2 (lib.).
  1. Adoption. I. Williams, Mary E., 1960– . II. Opposing viewpoints series.
  HV875A3185 2006
  362.734--dc22

                                              2006043350

Printed in the United States of America
10 9 8 7 6 5 4 3 2 1

Contents

Why Consider Opposing Viewpoints?   11

Introduction   14

Chapter 1: Should Adoption Be Encouraged?

Chapter Preface   19

1. Adoption Is Beneficial   21
   J.C. Willke

2. Adoption Can Be Harmful   26
   Lori Carangelo

3. Adoption Should Be Promoted over Abortion   34
   Annie H.

4. Adoption Should Not Be Promoted over Abortion   38
   Adam Pertman, interviewed by Cynthia Dailard

5. Single Mothers Should Give Up Their Children   43
   for Adoption
   Family in America

6. Single Mothers Should Not Necessarily Give Up   48
   Their Children for Adoption
   Heather Lowe

Periodical Bibliography   55

Chapter 2: Whose Rights Should Be Protected in the Adoption Process?

Chapter Preface   57

1. The Rights of Birth Mothers Should Be Protected   59
   Origins Canada

2. The Rights of Birth Fathers Should Be Protected   70
   Gary Clapton

3. The Rights of Adoptive Parents Should   78
   Be Protected
   Jeff Jacoby

4. The Rights of Adopted Children Should   82
   Be Protected
   National Council for Adoption

Periodical Bibliography   89

Chapter 3: What Types of Adoption Should Be Encouraged?

Chapter Preface   91

1. Transracial Adoption Should Be Encouraged   93
   Arlene Istar Lev

2. Same-Race Adoption Should Be Encouraged   102
   National Association of Black Social Workers

3. International Adoption Should Be Supported   113
   Debbie Spivack

4. International Adoption Is Harmful   122
   Tobias Hubinette

5. Homosexuals Should Have the Right to Adopt   131
   Part I: Adam Pertman; Part II: American Academy
   of Pediatrics

6. Homosexuals Should Not Have the Right to Adopt   139
   Robert H. Knight

7. Embryo Adoption Should Be Encouraged   147
   Jonathan Imbody

8. Supporting Embryo Adoption Is Hypocritical   153
   Michael Ennis

Periodical Bibliography   162

Chapter 4: Which Adoption Policies Should Be Supported?

Chapter Preface   **164**

1. Open Adoption Policies Should Be Supported   **166**
   Brenda Romanchik

2. Open Adoptions Are Not for Everyone   **172**
   Anita L. Allen

3. Adoption Records Should Be Unsealed   **180**
   Lorraine Dusky

4. Unsealing Adoption Records Could Have Negative   **186**
   Consequences
   Mary Kenny

5. Foster Care and Adoption Are Preferable to   **192**
   Family Preservation
   Connie Marshner

6. Family Preservation Is Preferable to Foster Care   **201**
   and Adoption
   National Coalition for Child Protection Reform

Periodical Bibliography   **207**

For Further Discussion   **208**

Organizations to Contact   **211**

Bibliography of Books   **215**

Index   **219**

Why Consider Opposing Viewpoints?

> *"The only way in which a human being can make some approach to knowing the whole of a subject is by hearing what can be said about it by persons of every variety of opinion and studying all modes in which it can be looked at by every character of mind. No wise man ever acquired his wisdom in any mode but this."*
>
> John Stuart Mill

In our media-intensive culture it is not difficult to find differing opinions. Thousands of newspapers and magazines and dozens of radio and television talk shows resound with differing points of view. The difficulty lies in deciding which opinion to agree with and which "experts" seem the most credible. The more inundated we become with differing opinions and claims, the more essential it is to hone critical reading and thinking skills to evaluate these ideas. Opposing Viewpoints books address this problem directly by presenting stimulating debates that can be used to enhance and teach these skills. The varied opinions contained in each book examine many different aspects of a single issue. While examining these conveniently edited opposing views, readers can develop critical thinking skills such as the ability to compare and contrast authors' credibility, facts, argumentation styles, use of persuasive techniques, and other stylistic tools. In short, the Opposing Viewpoints Series is an ideal way to attain the higher-level thinking and reading skills so essential in a culture of diverse and contradictory opinions.

In addition to providing a tool for critical thinking, Opposing Viewpoints books challenge readers to question their own strongly held opinions and assumptions. Most people form their opinions on the basis of upbringing, peer pressure, and personal, cultural, or professional bias. By reading carefully balanced opposing views, readers must directly confront new ideas as well as the opinions of those with whom they disagree. This is not to simplistically argue that everyone who reads opposing views will—or should—change his or her opinion. Instead, the series enhances readers' understanding of their own views by encouraging confrontation with opposing ideas. Careful examination of others' views can lead to the readers' understanding of the logical inconsistencies in their own opinions, perspective on why they hold an opinion, and the consideration of the possibility that their opinion requires further evaluation.

Evaluating Other Opinions

To ensure that this type of examination occurs, Opposing Viewpoints books present all types of opinions. Prominent spokespeople on different sides of each issue as well as well-known professionals from many disciplines challenge the reader. An additional goal of the series is to provide a forum for other, less known, or even unpopular viewpoints. The opinion of an ordinary person who has had to make the decision to cut off life support from a terminally ill relative, for example, may be just as valuable and provide just as much insight as a medical ethicist's professional opinion. The editors have two additional purposes in including these less known views. One, the editors encourage readers to respect others' opinions—even when not enhanced by professional credibility. It is only by reading or listening to and objectively evaluating others' ideas that one can determine whether they are worthy of consideration. Two, the inclusion of such viewpoints encourages the important critical thinking skill of objectively evaluating an author's credentials and bias. This evaluation will illuminate an author's reasons for taking a particular stance on an issue and will aid in readers' evaluation of the author's ideas.

It is our hope that these books will give readers a deeper understanding of the issues debated and an appreciation of the complexity of even seemingly simple issues when good and honest people disagree. This awareness is particularly important in a democratic society such as ours in which people enter into public debate to determine the common good. Those with whom one disagrees should not be regarded as enemies but rather as people whose views deserve careful examination and may shed light on one's own.

Thomas Jefferson once said that "difference of opinion leads to inquiry, and inquiry to truth." Jefferson, a broadly educated man, argued that "if a nation expects to be ignorant and free . . . it expects what never was and never will be." As individuals and as a nation, it is imperative that we consider the opinions of others and examine them with skill and discernment. The Opposing Viewpoints Series is intended to help readers achieve this goal.

David L. Bender and Bruno Leone,
Founders

Introduction

"There is a new affirmation of the family that recognizes both blood kinship and adoptive kinship."

—*Barbara Melosh,* Strangers and Kin: The American Way of Adoption

Adoption has existed since antiquity. As far back as the Babylonian Code of Hammurabi of 1780 B.C., various societies have legally sanctioned the transfer of children to nurturers who are not biologically related to them. In some cases, as in the ancestor-oriented Shinto religion, adoption fulfilled religious requirements by enabling adoptees to perform important lineage rituals for childless families. In other cases, adoption allowed powerful dynasties to maintain political supremacy. Julius Caesar, for example, continued his reign by adopting his nephew Octavian, who became Caesar Augustus. Thus adoption has long fulfilled social and familial needs in many parts of the world.

Not all societies have always endorsed adoption, however. In England and several other European nations, the practice of primogeniture, in which land is always inherited by a family's eldest biological son, predominated for hundreds of years. Inheritance laws that emphasized bloodlines became the norm in much of the Western world, allowing few opportunities for a family to "live on" through adopted children. In England, furthermore, the only way for a child born out of wedlock to become an heir was through the process of "legitimation." In these instances a jury made decisions about legitimacy on a case by case basis. Favorable outcomes were rare.

The significance attached to legitimacy created unique dilemmas for illegitimate children in pre–twentieth century England, where there was no legal form of adoption. Orphaned or illegitimate children who were not under the care of relatives or friends had to fend for themselves as thieves, beggars, or prostitutes. Although the Elizabethan Poor Law of 1601 formally provided assistance for the orphaned, a stigma against unwed mothers and illegitimate children remained entrenched. Since formal adoption was unavailable, illegitimate children might be abandoned, sold, placed in indentured servitude, or sent to live in foster homes and almshouses.

The United States was the first Western nation to establish adoption reforms that took into account the interests of the child. Thomas Jefferson laid the groundwork for a philosophy favoring adoption by helping to eliminate primogeniture in Virginia in 1783. In 1851 Massachusetts passed "An Act to Provide for the Adoption of Children," considered by many experts to be the first modern adoption law. By the end of the nineteenth century, some states had passed laws requiring the investigation of couples seeking to adopt children. For the most part, however, U.S. adoption remained an informal and unregulated practice until the twentieth century.

States first began passing laws that required confidential, or closed, adoptions in the early 1900s. In 1917 Minnesota became the first state mandating that the information about an adoptee's birth history be kept sealed. By the 1950s nearly every other state had followed Minnesota's lead. At a time when society frowned on unwed mothers and held illegitimate children, or "bastards," in contempt, closed adoption was seen as a way to protect the privacy of the adoptee, the birth mother, and the adoptive family. Adoptive parents had no access to information about the biological parents of their adopted children, nor did birth parents have any way to find out about the children they had given up. Experts also believed that eliminating all connections to the birth parents would ensure that the adoptive family assumed all parental rights and obligations in regard to the child.

By the 1970s, however, critics began challenging the practice of closed adoption. For one thing, changing sexual mores had removed some of the stigma associated with unwed pregnancy, and birth mothers began to seek involvement in choosing the parents of their children. A growing number of adults who had been adopted demanded access to their birth records and biological heritage. Perhaps most significantly, studies revealed that many people—particularly adoptees and birth mothers—suffered psychological problems connected to the imposed secrecy of the closed adoption process. Some biological parents, knowing that they would never see their children again, experienced prolonged grief and anxiety. Some adoptees encountered a sense of rejection as well as difficulties with identity development. In response to these insights, several adoption agencies began to allow birth mothers to participate in the selection of adoptive parents for their children. This new approach to child placement soon evolved into open adoption, in which information about birth parents and adoptive parents is disclosed to all parties.

Today, more than half of the adoptions certified within the United States are open—that is, birth parents, adoptive parents, and adoptive children have complete identifying information and ongoing contact over the years. In addition, some families opt for "semi-open" arrangements, which may involve communication with birth parents through letters and photos and/or a limited number of face-to-face meetings. Advocates of open adoption maintain that it is the healthiest choice in a society that supports disclosure and honest communication. It is not problem free, however. Open adoption supporters Kathleen Silber and Patricia Martinez Dorner acknowledge that birth parents and adoptive parents may have "differences in lifestyles and values" that could lead to serious disagreements about child-rearing. Some critics also maintain that including birth parents as part of an "extended family" could weaken the bond between the child and the adoptive family.

Balancing the interests of adoptees, birth parents, and adoptive parents will continue to be a challenge as choices within the adoption process increase. *Opposing Viewpoints: Adoption* includes the following chapters: Should Adoption Be Encouraged? Whose Rights Should Be Protected in the Adoption Process? What Types of Adoption Should Be Encouraged? Which Adoption Policies Should Be Supported? Authors examine such compelling issues as transracial parenting, gay and lesbian parenting, international adoptions, and family preservation.

OPPOSING
VIEWPOINTS®
SERIES

CHAPTER 1

Should Adoption Be Encouraged?

Chapter Preface

Adoption is commonly seen as the best alternative for a woman with an unplanned pregnancy who wishes neither to have an abortion nor raise a child. Many child welfare experts also view adoption as the healthiest solution for children who have been subjected to abuse or neglect and for youths who have been in the foster care system. Children who are adopted have the opportunity to experience a stable family life with parents who want and love them, adoption advocates maintain. Furthermore, advocates argue, adoption enables those who cannot give birth the chance to nurture troubled or needy children by becoming parents.

Some experts, however, have serious reservations about adoption. These critics claim that terminating the biological relationship between mother and child has long-term negative consequences. According to clinical psychologist Nancy Verrier, an infant's experience of the loss of its natural mother creates a "primal wound" in the psyche. This wound can lead to problems with self-esteem, identity development, trust, loyalty, and intimacy, she points out. Antiadoption activist Joss Shawyer agrees, stating that "the shock experienced by newborn babies separated from their mothers . . . contributes to the high rates of psychiatric disturbances found amongst adopted people." Other critics also assert that most adoptions of older children are not necessary and could be prevented by increased efforts to assist biological families. Family law attorney Nanette Schoor suggests that "help should take the form of 'family preservation' funding programs that assist families before their children are removed."

Adoption advocates grant that adoptees may experience challenges related to their adoption, but they contend that these challenges are not insurmountable or inevitable. According to a study conducted by Cheryl Kodjo, adopted adoles-

cents report more emotional distress and family disconnected-
ness than their nonadopted counterparts. However, adopted
teens do not engage in more high-risk behaviors (such as
drug use, violence, or suicide attempts) than nonadopted
teens, nor do adoptees have more negative experiences as
young adults than nonadoptees, Kodjo reports. The National
Council for Adoption, moreover, insists that adoption is beneficial: "Adoption is healthy, satisfying, and good for adopted
persons, not an enduring challenge to identity and wholeness.
The adopted person may have additional questions and curiosities to sort out, but adoption is not a psychological burden
or pathology. . . . Adoption is the way one joined one's family,
not a defining characteristic or lifelong process."

These conflicting views on the benefits and drawbacks of
adoption are further examined in the following chapter, in
which analysts debate whether adoption should be promoted
over single parenthood or abortion.

| "*Adopted kids do very well.*"

Adoption Is Beneficial

J.C. Willke

Adoption benefits children born outside of marriage as well as unmarried pregnant women, argues J.C. Willke in the following viewpoint. Children who were adopted as infants often have higher levels of health, self-esteem, and family support when compared with their nonadopted counterparts, he points out. In addition, teenage mothers who put their babies up for adoption are more likely to continue their education and less likely to wind up in poverty or on public assistance. Willke, a physician, is president of the Life Issues Institute in Cincinnati, Ohio.

As you read, consider the following questions:

1. Why has the adoption rate declined, according to Willke?

2. According to the author, what percentage of adopted teenagers is psychologically healthy?

3. What did the Columbia University study of four hundred pregnant teenagers discover about single mothers who chose to give their babies up for adoption?

J.C. Willke, "Benefits of Adoption," *Life Issues Connector*, vol. 12, October 2003, p. 2. © Life Issues Institute, Inc. 2003. Reproduced by permission.

The number of out-of-wedlock births in the United States has peaked. It hit a record high of 1.3 million in 1999, but the adoption rate has still been declining. Forty years ago, almost 10% of all babies born to unwed mothers were placed in adoptive arms. By the middle of the '90s, it had fallen to one percent.

There are many reasons for this. The removal of the stigma of unwed motherhood in our society certainly was a big one. The campaign by the pro-abortion industry to discredit adoption is also a large factor. In addition, there are a lot of misconceptions out there, so let's look at a study of the impact on adopted children.

The Search Institute Study

A study by the Search Institute of over 700 families examined these children twelve to eighteen years after they were born and placed for adoption. Here's what the study showed:

- Adopted adolescents' self-esteem was as high or higher than their peers.

- Adopted adolescents are as deeply attached to their adoptive parents as their siblings who were not adopted.

- 95% of the parents said they had a very strong attachment to their adopted child.

- How many parents were divorced or separated? Only 11%. This compared to 28% of a cross-section nationally.

- 75% of adopted adolescents are psychologically healthy.

- Adopted adolescents report having as much support from family and friends as their non-adopted siblings have.

Another somewhat similar study compared adopted children with three other groups: children born out of wedlock and raised by a single mother; children raised by grandparents without their biologic parents; and children who live with both of their biologic parents. Among these three, how did the adopted children fare?

- They had superior home environments, more so than any of the other groups.

- They were in better health than children living with unmarried mothers and those living with grandparents.

- Access to medical care was similar to children in intact families, and better than the others.

- Children repeating a grade, being suspended or expelled from school—how did they do? Their numbers were the same as children in intact families, and their records were much better than children living with un-married mothers or living with grandparents.

So, what's the bottom-line here, friends? Adopted kids do very well.

Benefits for the Birth Mother

I have listed above some of the benefits that children placed for adoption have. Let's now look at the unwed mother her-self—the woman who unselfishly placed that child in another pair of loving arms.

There's a study from Planned Parenthood's Family Planning Perspectives of 270 unwed mothers. It reported that those young mothers who placed their babies for adoption had considerably more favorable social, economic and educational outcomes than did those who kept their babies and parented as single parents. Comparing the two groups, the study showed that those who placed their children for adoption were:

- More likely to finish vocational training and more likely to have educational aspirations.

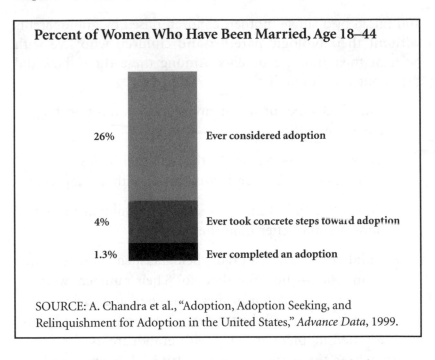

Percent of Women Who Have Been Married, Age 18–44

26%   Ever considered adoption

4%   Ever took concrete steps toward adoption

1.3%   Ever completed an adoption

SOURCE: A. Chandra et al., "Adoption, Adoption Seeking, and Relinquishment for Adoption in the United States," *Advance Data*, 1999.

- More likely to delay marriage and considerably less likely to have another out-of-wedlock pregnancy.

- More likely to be employed six to twelve months after giving birth and, across the board, almost all had higher household incomes.

Benefits for Pregnant Teens

Here's another study at Columbia University of over 400 pregnant teenagers. It checked them at six months and again at four years after giving birth. Again, those who placed their babies for adoption fared much better than single mothers who chose to parent their own child. In this study, mothers who placed their babies for adoption were:

- More likely to complete high school; more likely to attend college; more likely to have higher educational aspirations; more likely to be employed six months and four years after giving birth; and—a big one—more likely to be married.

- They were less likely to be on welfare. There were fewer of them who were cohabiting and fewer who had another out-of-wedlock pregnancy.

- Those who placed their babies were more likely to have greater overall satisfaction with their lives, including satisfaction with their work, finances and relationship with their partners.

- Finally, they were more likely to be optimistic about their own future. And, among this group, there were fewer women suffering from depression.

In summary, unwed mothers who carried their babies to term and placed them in loving arms for adoption scored higher, with greater satisfaction and with greater social stability on almost every level, that is, in comparison to the young mothers who kept their babies and proceeded to raise them as single mothers.

Remember, I'm not talking about every single mother. I'm talking about averages. Some single mothers do a bang-up job, and we owe them a great debt for what they can accomplish and do with their children.

> "What [is] seen in many adopted chil-
> dren is the beginning of a cycle of vio-
> lence against adopters or strangers or
> both."

Adoption Can Be Harmful

Lori Carangelo

*In the following viewpoint Lori Carangelo argues that all adop-
tees are at risk of a behavior disorder known as Adopted Child
Syndrome (ACS). This syndrome—which may include pathological lying, stealing, learning disabilities, relationship difficulties, and antisocial behaviors—stems from the broken bond between a child and his or her biological mother, the author
contends. The loss of the biological mother creates a primal
wound in the psyche that can eventually cause emotional disturbances and violent rage, Carangelo asserts. Carangelo is president of Americans for Open Records, an online network concerned with family rights issues.*

As you read, consider the following questions:

1. What are the eight most commonly noted symptoms of
   Adopted Child Syndrome, according to Carangelo?

2. In what cases has Adopted Child Syndrome been cited
   as a legal defense?

Lori Carangelo, "Adopted Child Syndrome (ACS): Its History and Relevance Today,"
www.amfor.net/acs/, August 2005. Reproduced by permission.

3. What is the connection between serial killers and adoption, in Carangelo's view?

According to public opinion polls, most Americans agree that adoption is at least a "risk factor" to a child's developmental, behavioral and academic development. The belief that adoption has a psychology of its own is evidenced by clinical studies amassed both prior to and since the late 1940s when the states began making adoptees' origins secret.

That adoptees are prone to specific behaviors referred to as "Adopted Child Syndrome," says famed attorney and Harvard Law Professor, Alan Dershowitz, is just another "abuse excuse" to avoid reponsibility for their actions, including felony crimes. But this is the same Alan Dershowitz who, in his op-ed piece in the *LA Times*, suggested using "Torture Warrants"—court ordered to control what Dershowitz calls the "inevitable" use of torture by U.S. law enforcement in the "war on terrorism." He claims torture is "constitutional," regardless that it is also detrimental to a democratic society. He rationalizes that its sanctioning by warrant would make it more accountable and transparent. "If we are to have torture," he argues, "it should be authorized by the law." Notwithstanding that falsification of sealed birth records, and adoption itself, have never been deemed "constitutional" or democratic, Dershowitz seems to be missing the point of our profiling people who are victims of adoption abuse, not as an "excuse," but as a "reason" for the prevalance of sociopathology and violent crime among those whose lives were forever manipulated by adoption politics and lawyers "in their best interests."

Adopted Child Syndrome

In 1953, Jean Paton, . . . a social worker and adoptee, conducted the first studies on families involved in sealed adoptions under the name "The Life History Center," in Philadelphia. In the June 1955 edition of the *Western Journal of Surgery*, Paton described "passive, hostile and dependent behaviors" in an adopted boy—behaviors she later defined and which would later be more widely known as "Adopted Child Syndrome." Her studies revealed confused, damaged children and families due to this secrecy based on ever-changing social work theory and political expediency. Subsequently, terminology such as "slave psychology" was applied to the adoptee "because he feels he must submit to the will of his adopters as a reflection of what they have done for him.". . .

In 1978, Dr. David Kirschner coined the term "Adopted Child Syndrome" as underlying "Dissociative Disorder," in his paper, "Son of Sam and the Adopted Child Syndrome.". . .

In the 1980s, adoptees who exhibited "Attachment Disorder" were further categorized as a "sub-set spectrum" of adoptees who, to varying degrees, exhibit eight specific antisocial Adopted Child Syndrome (ACS) behaviors—according to noted psychologists, Kirschner, Sorosky, Schecter, Carlson, Simmons, Work, Goodman, Silverstein, Mandell, Menlove, Simon, Senturia, Offord, Aponti, Cross and others. However, the "spectrum" is never defined, so it is argued that all adoptees are at risk due to the complexities of adoptees' dual identities and secret pasts. Although [some critics] referred to ACS as "malarkey" in the press, psychiatrist David Cooke said "Adopted Child Syndrome is simply a new name for a phenomenon that has been observed since the 1950's" (by Paton). The ACS behaviors most commonly referred to are:

- conflict with authority (for example truancy);

- preoccupation with excessive fantasy;

- pathological lying;

- stealing;

- running away (from home, school, group homes, situations);

- learning difficulties, under-achievement, over-achievement;

- lack of impulse control (acting out, promiscuity, sex crimes);

- fascination with fire, fire-setting

By 1982, in children diagnosed with Attention Deficit Disorder (ADD) for hyperactivity, a 17% rate of non-relative adoption was found—or eight times the rate for non-adopted children—and it was estimated that 23% of all adopted children would have ADD. Today that percentage is much higher. As Jean Paton pointed out, "Do you have to be truant, or drop out of school, steal, get into juvenile detention homes, in order for people to realize that you need to have someone tell you about your origins?" Apparently the answer is still YES.

Adoptees at Risk

Years laters Kirschner still maintained:

> In twenty-five years of practice I have seen hundreds of adoptees, most adopted in infancy. In case after case, I have observed what I have come to call the Adopted Child Syndrome, which may include pathological lying, stealing, truancy, manipulation, shallowness of attachment, provocation of parents and other authorities, threatened or actual running away, promiscuity, learning problems, fire-setting, and increasingly serious antisocial behavior, often leading to court custody. It may include an extremely negative or grandiose self-image, low frustration tolerance, and an absence of normal guilt or anxiety. . . .

Kirschner concludes his paper with "Finally, I believe that *most adoptees* have the same emotional vulnerabilities that are seen in dramatic form in the Adopted Child Syndrome, and that *all adoptees* are at risk."

The Primal Wound

What the [adopted] child has missed is the security and serenity of oneness with the person who gave birth to him, a
continuum of bonding from prenatal to postnatal life. This
is a profound connection for which the adoptee forever
yearns. It is this yearning which leaves him often feeling
hopeless, helpless, empty, and alone. In working with adoptees, it is apparent that no matter what happens a month, a
year, or several years in the future, that period immediately
after birth, when the infant has made the transition from
the warm, fluid, dark security of the womb to the cold,
bright, alien world of postnatal life, is a crucial period. It is
a time when a baby needs to be in proximity to his mother
in order to find the world safe and welcoming instead of
confusing, uncaring, and hostile. At that time the mother is
the whole world for the baby, and his connection to her is
essential to his sense of well-being and wholeness.

It is my belief, therefore, that *the severing of that connection between the adopted child and his birthmother causes a
primal or narcissistic wound, which affects the adoptee's sense
of Self and often manifests in a sense of loss, basic mistrust,
anxiety and depression, emotional and/or behavioral problems, and difficulties in relationships with significant others.*

Nancy Newton Verrier,
The Primal Wound: Understanding the Adopted Child, *1993.*

In 1992, David M Brodzinsky, Marshall D Schechter & Robin
Marantz Henig, authored *Being Adopted: The Lifelong Search
for Self.* Using their combined total of 55 years experience in
clinical and research work with adoptees and their families,
the authors use the voices of adoptees themselves to trace how
adoption is experienced over a lifetime. Studies have shown

that being adopted can affect many aspects of adoptees' lives, from relationships with adoptive parents to bonds with their own children.

Adoption and Violence

On September 23, 1992, Attorney Donald Humphrey, himself an adoptee, called attention to the Syndrome as a factor in cases where children murdered their adopters in "Violence in Adoption," a talk he gave at a conference of the American Adoption Congress.

In 1993 and 1994, the Syndrome was used as a defense in two cases of juvenile adoptees who murdered their adopters. Kirschner, a child psychologist, identified the Syndrome as a contributing factor with regard to Patrick DeGellecke who was 14 when he killed his adopters by setting fire to their home.

In "Heikkila," *Courier News* . . . Laurence Arnold added that the Syndrome is further characterized by "an absence of normal guilt or anxiety about one's deeds" and news stories that characterize young adoptees who killed their adopters as displaying "no emotion" or having "no remorse" support this. The *New York Times* account of Matthew Heikkila's crime, "How the Adoption System Ignites a Fire," by Betty Jean Lifton . . . cites Kirschner as well as psychiatrist Arthur Sorosky, who helped set the precedent in the DeGellecke case with the Adopted Child Syndrome defense.

Adoptees including Larry Swartz (Maryland), Patrick Campbell (Connecticut), and Tammy and Kathryn Tomassoni (Arizona), now adults, were tried and convicted "as juveniles" for the murders of their respective adopters but also are among the very few adoptees who, having served their sentences, were released from prison. They never killed again and were reportedly living "normal" lives. Swartz, who married and had a child, was well liked by the community who called him a caring person; he was only 37 when he died unexpectedly of a heart attack in 2004.... Other adoptees, such as Heikkila and Marty Tankleff, who were juveniles when they murdered their adopters (in Connecticut and New York, respectively), were neverthless convicted "as adults" and remain in prison.

A Wound to the Psyche

Dr. Patrick J. Callahan, trained in both death investigation and psychological profiling, (Forensic, Educational and Neuropsychology and Child, Adult and Family Psychotherapy in Yorba Linda, California, and who has consulted on high profile cases such as the Jon Benet Ramsey murder case), offers the most intriguing and probably the most accurate assessment of the psychological dynamics of adoptees—particularly adoptees who commit violent crimes. He asserts that adoption, whether legal or illegal, is a dysfunction of kinship, and that the adoptee perceives many people in his world as "strangers." What he has seen in many adopted children is the beginning of a cycle of violence against adopters or strangers or both.... He believes there may be a reaction experienced by the adopted child that is the most primitive wound to the psyche, and is experienced at the very essence of his/her humanity even in adulthood. By and of itself, the adoptee's specific loss of the most elementary biological kinship, in the process known as adoption, may cause "paleo-psychological regression" experienced as uncontrollable rage deep from within his/her own ancient history which, when focused, may find its end as predatory violence....

Explaining Adoptee Behavior

Until the book, *Chosen Children*, and AmFOR's [Americans for Open Records] web page at http://AdoptedKillers.com made this information available, free on Internet, no one work had linked the majority of serial killers and others by the abnormality of their adoptive status. Increasingly, profilers, psychologists, sociologists, educators, journalists, script writers, defense attorneys and other researchers understand and explain adoptees' behaviors in the context of their adoptions.

> *"There was no way I was going to violently kill my baby for my personal temporary comfort."*

Adoption Should Be Promoted over Abortion

Annie H.

In the following viewpoint Annie H. describes her experience of giving up her baby son for adoption during her college years. Annie knew that she had the option of raising the child herself or of having an abortion, but she realized these were not viable choices. Although she experienced sadness after relinquishing her child, Annie believes that abortion is akin to murder and that such a decision creates much deeper heartache for a woman. By giving birth and choosing adoption, Annie feels that she has given the gift of life, stability, and family to her child. Annie H. is a medical professional who lives in North Carolina.

As you read, consider the following questions:

1. Why did Annie H. decide not to keep her baby?

2. How did Annie's family and co-workers react to her decision to give her baby up for adoption?

3. What kind of relationship does the author have with the son she relinquished?

Hi. My name is Annie H., and I am a "birthmother." My son was conceived during my first semester of college, as I was studying pre-med and running cross-country; naive, sure that "it-can't-happen-to-me." Shortly after breaking up with "Bob," I began to fear I was pregnant. Later, my roommate accompanied me to Birthright of Memphis for a pregnancy test. Sure enough, I was seven weeks along. I was in shock; I was a "good" person—and I was pregnant.

Choosing Adoption

Ironically, when I started having sex with Bob, I knew that if I got pregnant, I would choose adoption. I realized that I needed to place my baby for adoption, not just for myself, but for the baby—my baby, the living, growing person that was being created in me. I knew there were other options: keeping the baby, or abortion, which I have opposed since "teenhood": there was no way I was going to violently kill my baby for my personal temporary comfort. As for raising him myself, I feared that as a single parent I just couldn't be enough. Bob was out of the picture, and although he knew I was pregnant, he denied his involvement, and we haven't spoken since.

End of semester, and I moved home, started community college, and started on the road to adoption. At first I felt like a "flunkie," but that semester I met many wonderful people who walked me down a path I don't think I could have crawled down alone. Meanwhile, I started meeting with a social worker at Catholic Charities to talk about all the emotional, social, and legal ramifications of placing a baby for adoption.

There were some dark moments, too, like when my mom and I fought or when Bob's mother tried to scare me out of adoption. One day, I was discussing my baby's future with a friend when a co-worker walked up and added, "If you're going to give your baby away, why didn't you just have an abortion?" I don't remember if I could even speak, but those words still bring a sour taste to my mouth. She was talking about my baby, my son, who bruised my ribs with his kicking, had the hiccups at least once a day, who kept me alive to keep him alive.

The Feeling of New Life

I cannot express the exuberance of feeling new life growing within you. I first felt the baby kicking at four months. FOUR MONTHS! What a miracle.

And I could not believe the number of wonderful couples who sent me letters, wanting to adopt my baby! Eventually I picked my roommate's oldest sister and her husband to be my baby's family. They were more wonderful than I could've imagined, providing support, encouragement, and a joyful ear to discuss the baby's growth. Together, we dreamed up the life for "our" son. One fun night we stayed up late, brainstorming names for "our" baby. The time went so quickly—and before we knew it, his birthday had arrived. At 10:42 p.m., I gave birth to the most beautiful baby to ever join this world. His mom says I decided on his name, but I don't really remember—I was too excited to finally meet this person growing inside me.

The next morning I retrieved my son from the hospital nursery, to bid him farewell. I laid him next to me, wrapped myself around him, and just looked at my perfect, beautiful baby.

A Manageable Heartache

I don't know how to describe the emptiness I felt when my son and I went our separate ways. Many people told me to think about it as if he had died, but he hadn't died. He was alive, living a wonderful life that I had given him. Although my heart ached some, it could never have ached like the ache of sacrificinig an unborn life to abortion. I cannot imagine the pain, grief, guilt, and hollowness that would cause a woman. With the comfort of knowing that I had done the

Asay. Reprinted by permission of Chuck Asay and Creators Syndicate.

right thing, the best thing for my son, life slowly started to get back to normal, and my heart began its slow process of piecing itself back together. I resumed classes, began running again, and rejoined the choir. I am now a 25-year-old medical professional. But don't be disillusioned—my life will never be the same.

I have visited my son a few times since then. He is six now, still so beautiful, and so smart and talented. We exchange pictures and a card every Christmas, so I KNOW this. Although some of the feelings of letting my baby go remains, I think it's okay, because that is part of what I have left of my son. But moreover, I have the joy and pride of knowing that I gave my beautiful, smart, loving son the best life I could, a stable family life with a mommy and a daddy, and everything he could ever need. And no one will ever take that away from me.

| "*Information about all options (including abortion) should be presented to pregnant women.*"

Adoption Should Not Be Promoted over Abortion

Adam Pertman, interviewed by Cynthia Dailard

In the following viewpoint Adam Pertman discusses the need for health care providers to give pregnant women unbiased counseling regarding the options that are available to them. Federal law requires that women be given information about adoption, parenting, and abortion—and no choice is to be given preference over the other, Pertman points out. Certain counselor training programs, however, actively promote adoption. He argues that such programs are unethical because they do not aim to empower women to make the choice that is best for them. Pertman is executive director of the Even B. Donaldson Adoption Institute and the author of the book Adoption Nation. *He is interviewed by Cynthia Dailard, a senior public policy associate at the Alan Guttmacher Institute in Washington, D.C.*

As you read, consider the following questions:

1. What is the Infant Adoption Awareness Act?

2. In Pertman's opinion, what is wrong with the counselor training provided by the National Council for Adoption?

Cynthia Dailard with Adam Pertman, "An Adoption Expert Discusses Implementation of the Infant Adoption Awareness Act," *Guttmacher Report on Public Policy*, vol. 7, August 2004, p. 12-13. Reproduced by permission of Alan Guttmacher Institute.

3. How does openness in the adoption process affect abortion rates, according to the author?

C *ynthia Dailard: First of all, what is your professional opinion of the best-practices guidelines that were developed under the IAAA?*[1]

Adam Pertman: I think they were put together thoughtfully; if adhered to, they would be good for both women who choose adoption and women who choose another path. I think they are a positive step for putting adoption on a level playing field with the other options available to women who are not sure they want to—or are able to—parent their children. There appears to be a problem, however, with the implementation of these guidelines by the national grantee, the National Council for Adoption. NCFA is an umbrella organization for adoption agencies that are mostly Christian and Mormon—many of which have certain moral, religious and philosophical views that do not comport with the notion of presenting women facing an unintended pregnancy with all of their options in a neutral, unbiased way.

Counselor Training

What do you believe are the major problems with NCFA's national curriculum?

First, let me stress that I am sure many if not most of the trainers—especially those with the more regional grantees—work hard to get it right, whatever guidelines are on paper. But the curriculum itself seems to violate the spirit and the letter of the law because it does not address the concept or techniques of nondirective counseling. For instance, good practice should start with a discussion of legal requirements, professional standards for options counseling and guidance

1. The Infant Adoption Awareness Act, signed into law in 2000, authorized grants to train health care providers to counsel pregnant women about all of their legal options.

for implementing the standards in practice. It also should follow the regulatory and ethical mandates to offer counseling and obtain consent before actually providing it. But all that is barely addressed in the national training curriculum.

Furthermore, the training curriculum presents only parenting or adoption as pregnancy resolution options, without recognizing—as the law dictates—that information about all options (including abortion) should be presented to pregnant women. And the information and the manner in which it is presented appear intended to convey the sense that adoption is the only right choice; that's not nondirective by any definition.

Minimizing the Abortion Option

Here's an example of how the way in which adoption is presented is so important: The curriculum presents the best interests of the "child" as paramount; that sounds just right and, in the adoption world, it's accepted as a given. But invariably refers to children who need homes, not ones who are not yet born. No professional standards of practice advise physicians and counselors to recommend to pregnant women that they weigh the best interests of their fetuses and as yet unidentified adoptive parents on a par with their own. This perspective implicitly furthers an agenda aimed at minimizing the option of abortion and perhaps even the option of parenting by the biological mother.

Finally, the curriculum sometimes encourages the promotion of adoption actively, both implicitly and explicitly, by making value judgments and selectively presenting information and research. Additionally, it propagates basic misperceptions about pregnant women and birth mothers, and thus perpetuates the stigmas associated with unplanned pregnancy, single parenting and adoption.

Counseling Standards

Federal regulations for the Title X family planning program require pregnancy counselors to "offer pregnant women the opportunity to be provided information and counseling regarding each of the following options: prenatal care and delivery; infant care; foster care, or adoption; and pregnancy termination." If such information and counseling is requested, counselors must "provide neutral, factual information and nondirective counseling on each of the options, and referral upon request, except with respect to any option(s) about which the pregnant woman indicates she does not wish to receive such information and counseling." The Department of Health and Human Services also elaborates that "nondirective" means that counselors "may not steer or direct clients toward selecting any option."

Cynthia Dailard, Guttmacher Report on Public Policy, *August 2004.*

The Need to Avoid Bias

What should be taught as part of these trainings?

Whether or not to choose adoption is an extremely difficult decision with profound lifelong implications, so it should be made thoughtfully and carefully. Pregnancy counselors need to recognize this and be as humanely respectful as possible. They need to be scrupulously conscientious not just in what information they impart, but also how they impart it. Their tone is very important, for example. They need to consider whether they make women feel empowered to make the decision that is right for them or whether they bring bias to the table or are directive and disrespectful. This means that adoption awareness training should emphasize that counselors must maintain a level playing field with respect to adoption, as well as the other options available to pregnant women. My experience working with some of the more regional program grantees—who have chosen not to follow many aspects of the national curriculum because they do not share NCFA's views—suggests they are doing a very good job on this front.

Ultimately, a counselor needs to be able to give a woman the best available information about adoption and let her make her decision. The government's role should be to help ensure that this is how the process works.

Do you have other concerns relating to these trainings?

I do. A major one that is too seldom discussed is not just whether adoption is being presented in a nondirective way, but also *what kind* of adoption is being presented. The type of adoption that the NCFA curriculum promotes is the old-style, closed, secretive and still-stigmatized form that is no longer accepted by most adoption practitioners, who favor greater honesty, and openness in the process. Often, NCFA promotes closed adoption in the guise of "protecting" women. It also frames this discussion in the context of the abortion debate: If a woman is not guaranteed secrecy in her adoption, NCFA says, then she will choose abortion instead. This view is shared by some of the congressional authors of the IAAA. It is an attitude, however, that is disrespectful of women and does not reflect reality. Research simply shows it is not true. In states where there is openness relating to adoption, abortion rates are lower. Openness in adoption has occurred because birth mothers have insisted on it. They want to know what happens to their baby. So, there is a direct link to abortion in all of this.

| "Adopted children enjoy a number of advantages over children in long-term foster care and over children living with birth mothers."

Single Mothers Should Give Up Their Children for Adoption

Family in America

In the following viewpoint the editors of Family in America *contend that adopted children fare better than children who are raised by unwed mothers or children who live in foster homes and institutions. Research reveals that children raised in adoptive homes are more socially and intellectually developed when compared with their nonadopted counterparts. In addition, the authors maintain that an adoptive home provides a healing environment for children who were exposed to illegal drugs in the womb or who suffered abuse or neglect early in life. The* Family in America *is published by the Howard Center, a research and advocacy organization that supports the traditional two-parent family.*

As you read, consider the following questions:

1. According to a study of Romanian adoptees cited by the authors, which adoptees show the most favorable outcomes?

"The Adopted Child," *Family in America (New Research Section)*, September 2002, p. 3-4. Reproduced by permission.

2. What percentage of drug-exposed adoptees earn good grades, according to *Family in America?*

3. What accounts for the success of adopted children, in the authors' view?

A s the stigma attaching to illegitimacy has faded, more and more unwed mothers have chosen to keep their children rather than place them for adoption. The results for children of this trend may not be favorable. In an article recently published in *Early Human Development,* researcher Dana E. Johnson of the University of Minnesota surveys international research on adoption conducted over the last thirty years, research documenting the positive effects of adoption.

The Advantages of Adoption

For instance, a recent Swedish study cited by Johnson tracked adopted children from birth to young adulthood, revealing that adopted children enjoy a number of advantages over children in long-term foster care and over children living with birth mothers who originally had registered for adoption, but subsequently changed their minds and kept their babies. Although the Swedish study did show that adopted adolescents have "lower adjustment scores and lower mean grades than classmates," it also found that adjustment and academic performance was even "more problematic" among the foster children and among the adolescents living with birth mothers. And while "young men who remained with their birth mothers or were in long-term foster care scored significantly lower than the control groups on most IQ subtests," the young men who had been adopted had IQ scores that were "the same" as those of controls.

Similar advantages of adoption stand out in a British study comparing adults who had been adopted as children with adults from similar birth circumstances who had not. In the British study, researchers found that "at age 33, both men and

Adoption Versus Single-Parenting

Until thirty years ago the better options for unmarried pregnant women—marriage and adoption—held their own. From 1965 to 1973, however, Washington overrode state and local preferences and installed a bad choice, single-parenting, as a fundamental economic right, and a homicidal choice, abortion, as a fundamental legal right. Those preferences are still largely in effect, even though numerous research studies show that single-parenting is socially, economically, and psychologically destructive, but adoption of infants overwhelmingly works out well for babies, birthparents, and adoptive parents.

Marvin Olasky, National Review, *March 10, 1997.*

women in the birth comparison group were in less favorable social and material circumstances than the majority of the adopted children."

The Effects of Institutionalization

The pluses of adoption show up even more clearly when the focus shifts to children who have been institutionalized or who have been exposed in utero to illegal drugs.

Numerous studies have shown that institutionalization poses serious risks for children's normal development. But recent research shows clearly that adoption of children who have spent time in institutions can "reverse some of the deficits associated with early childhood institutionalization." Whether the focus is cognition, brain growth, behavioral abnormalities, or physical growth, institutionalized children show remarkable improvement if adopted. For instance, although a cognitive development in the "retarded range" is observed in more than half of the children (ages 0 to 42 months) leaving Romanian orphanages for adoption in the United Kingdom, these children make such "rapid progress" that when tested at age six, all age groups scored "in the normal range," with particularly favorable outcomes among those adopted when less than six months old. Indeed, "children adopted from institutional settings before 4–6 months of age appear to be virtually indistinguishable from domestic control groups in growth, cognitive skills, behavior and social skills, and attachment behavior."

Adoptees Who Were Exposed to Drugs

Recent research has also established favorable outcomes of adoption for children exposed to cocaine and other drugs in utero. In part because it "reduced the impact of parental drug exposure," adoption has been shown to yield "a better outcome than that of children exposed prenatally to cocaine and raised by their birth mothers." A long-term study of adopted children exposed to drugs in utero revealed that although these children were "more likely to have had difficulties within the educational system" (such as repeating a grade or being enrolled in a class for the learning disabled), they "generally functioned within the normal range and almost identically to non-drug-exposed adopted children in most areas." Almost three-quarters of the drug-exposed adopted children (71%) earned "good to excellent grades." Perhaps more important, more than 97% of the adoptive parents of these children "felt close to" their drug-exposed adopted child.

Available research also substantiates the power of an adoptive family to provide "a remarkable environment for healing emotional and physical trauma" for children who have suffered "severe neglect or abuse in early life."

The Best Social Program

No wonder that one leading researcher judges "adoption [to be] more favorable for children than any social program that I know," asserting that "the modest difficulties experienced by children who are adopted are far outweighed by the significant benefits they receive from having a permanent family."

Researchers have in fact traced the advantages of adopted children to "the adoptive parents' strong desire for the child, superior financial resources and a strong desire to build a relationship with the adopted child." Johnson further suggests that for the adopted child "an adoptive family is comparable to a birth family in its ability to create an environment that produces competent adults who can celebrate the joys and overcome the adversities of life."

| "Most experts on adoption agree that if a child can stay in his first family, he should."

Single Mothers Should Not Necessarily Give Up Their Children for Adoption

Heather Lowe

Heather Lowe, a writer in the field of public relations, is an adoption-reform activist. The following viewpoint is excerpted from a brochure Lowe wrote for pregnant women who are considering giving up their babies for adoption. In Lowe's opinion, adoption is traumatic for both the child and the birth mother. Adoptees often face a sense of abandonment, while birth mothers must deal with social rejection as well as the grief of relinquishing a child for whom they have developed maternal feelings. Lowe contends that a child should remain with his natural mother if possible and that birth mothers should be fully informed of the ramifications of adoption.

As you read, consider the following questions:

1. In Lowe's opinion, who are the people who really "count" in a birth mother's decision concerning adoption?

2. According to the author, how do Americans tend to view birth mothers?

3. What are some of the potential far-reaching effects of adoption, according to Lowe?

Because those of us in a crisis pregnancy are faced with stress, fear and loss, we're naturally prone to denial. That's one thing that makes thinking clearly about adoption so tricky. Another is that it's very hard to accurately imagine what adoption will be like. You really don't know until you've done it—and in many states, once you give your right to parent to someone else, there is no turning back. We at Concerned United Birthparents feel it's the duty of every birthparent to share what we wish we had known when we were considering adoption.

The words that follow are not intended to be anti-adoption. The fact is that adoption might well be the best plan for you and your child—but in order to be a truly good thing, it needs to be a well-considered decision, made at least twice—once before the birth, once after. Your decision will not be fully informed unless you hear the negative aspects of adoption as well as positive. Following are the most common regrets birthparents have voiced.

Family Preservation

"I wish I had known that family preservation should come first." Most experts on adoption agree that if a child can stay in his first family, he should. Family separation is traumatic for everyone involved, and if there is a way to keep the mother and child together, it should be found. Single parenthood is *not* inherently bad. Some people make excellent single parents, while others don't yet have the necessary skills.

Adoption is a permanent solution to an often temporary problem. For instance, consider how you will feel if you relinquish due to money reasons, and six months down the road, you have a good job that pays well. Or how you'll feel if you relinquish due to lack of family support, and the same people who did not want to help you raise your child are now saying, "We wish you'd kept the baby. We could have helped you." (Family members who are unhappy about your unplanned pregnancy will often do the most amazing turnaround once they meet the newborn baby.) Ask yourself why you're questioning your ability to parent: is it the opinions of others or your own deepest beliefs? Try to separate which of your problems are time-limited from those that seem here to stay. Some problems are insurmountable and may mean adoption is the answer, while others can be fixed if you know where to turn. Explore every alternative before considering adoption.

"I wish I had known the extent to which adopted children deal with issues of abandonment." Many adopted people, especially those in closed adoptions, report feeling abandoned by their birthmothers. While adoptees may be glad to have been adopted, they are not happy to have been relinquished. (In other words, they see their adoption as two separate events: being given up and being taken in.) It's very hard to accept that the most painful choice you make for your child might not be appreciated by them. There are no guarantees your child will like what you've done. Can you live with that? Don't fall into the "martyr" mindset that you are doing something beautiful and noble for your child—you might be disappointed if the eventual adult doesn't see it that way.

Choosing Adoption for the Wrong Reasons

"I wish I had known that I wasn't carrying my child for someone else, and that it wasn't my responsibility to help the infertile couples of the world." Ideally, adoption is supposed to be about giving a child a family, not giving a family a child, but sometimes that truth gets lost.

As a pregnant woman in a crisis situation, odds are you desperately want to make things better. You may be under

An Overshadowing Loss

For most birthmothers and many birthfathers, the loss of their child through adoption has overshadowed the rest of their lives. They have suffered largely in isolation, living with their lonely reality—a child was born to them whose whereabouts even as an adult may remain forever a mystery. Because of the stigmas associated with being a birthparent, even those friends and family who know about the baby rarely bring up the subject. This conspiracy of silence and secrecy, which began at the moment of the discovery of pregnancy, continued through to circumstances of the birth, to relinquishment, and afterward. . . . Many still today . . . are serving what they believe to be a lifelong sentence of silence and secrecy.

Jayne E. Schooler,
Journeys After Adoption: Understanding Lifelong Issues, *2002.*

enormous pressure, experiencing disapproval or shame. It's natural that you will want to "fix" things and earn approval once more, but it shouldn't be done by trying to make a prospective adoptive couples' dreams come true.

It can be emotionally wrenching to look through the profiles of hundreds of waiting couples, all of whom seem so "deserving" of parenthood when you aren't even sure if you are. You begin to feel sad for each of them. You start to see yourself as the one who can provide them with their most cherished desire. Furthermore, if your friends and family are not being supportive, the hopeful adoptive parents might be the only ones who are kind to you during your crisis. You may find yourself wanting to please them.

This is a mistake. *No matter how much you like the preadoptive parents, you must not put their feelings first.* Their hopes and dreams exist independently of you and your baby. If you entrust your baby to them in order to make them happy, you've chosen adoption for all the wrong reasons. If you decide to parent, they may be heartbroken, but they can always go on to find another child. It is not your responsibility to "fix" someone else's childlessness. The only people who should count in your decision are you and your child. In the words of birthmother Shannon Basore, "I can't fully feel that I did what was best for my child, because my focus at the time was providing this childless couple with a child of their own. And my grown child is angry about that."

Society's Views of Birthparents

"I wish I had known that society dislikes and fears birthparents." Americans have extremely unrealistic views of birthparents, painting us as either sinners or saints. Among the general public, a woman considering adoption is applauded as being admirably unselfish in pulling the needs of her child first. But once the mother actually surrenders her child, she is looked down upon. After all, "who could give away their own flesh and blood?"

As adoption author Jim Gritter has noted, nothing can prepare you for the plummet in your stock you will notice once you move from potential birthmother to birthmother. Often the very same people who said you were making a terrific, noble sacrifice while you were pregnant might now call you a heartless abandoner. What's even worse is that you confront this mental whiplash at a time when you are most vulnerable: grieving heavily, full of post-partum hormones, feeling completely alone in the world.

People in general don't understand the role of birthmother, and even birthmoms in the healthiest of open adoptions, who feel they made a great choice for their child, are sometimes unable to talk about it without experiencing judgement. Those uneducated about adoption issues tend to avert their eyes when you try to speak of your child, or whisper behind your back, saying hurtful things like, "I could never give my baby away."

Part of the reason the world fears birthmothers so much is that we show that the mother-child bond can be broken, at least outwardly and temporarily. If you choose to place your child for adoption, get prepared for a lifetime of being misunderstood by many and feared by others. . . .

The Strength of Mother-Love

"I wish I had known how much I was going to love my child." Predicting the strength of mother-love can be quite a difficult thing to do, especially for first-time mothers. Many new mothers express surprise at the overwhelming nature of the feeling—specially those who were encouraged to "disconnect" and "detach" from their baby in the womb, or who had troubled or non-existent relationships with the birthfather. Even mothers by rape can feel great love for their babies.

The feelings will take you by surprise. "I never imagined that I would miss or love my son as much as I do," says birthmother Su Parker. "I continue to wonder if I will ever find a complete healing in this," says Jennifer Maynard, also a birthmother, "It's almost like adoption is so *big* that you can only grasp little pieces at different times. But one thing I have no problem understanding is that I miss my son far more than I ever imagined.". . .

Far-Reaching Effects

"I wish I had known that the effects of adoption are so far-reaching." Let's look at the subsequent losses you might not have considered: Your parents will lose a grandchild. You may lose your relationship with your own grandchildren. Your nieces and nephews may have tough questions about why their cousin isn't with the family. Your subsequent children might fear that they will be given away. For medical or psy-

chological reasons, you could suffer secondary infertility and never be able to have another child. (Some studies suggest that secondary infertility among birthmothers can be as high as 40%.) You might lose your faith in intimate relationships, making it harder for you to trust and to love. Many of those you thought were your friends may judge and scorn you for your decision. Depression and grief could derail your productivity and your advancement in school or career.

These are just a few examples. Consider all the potential losses, not just the loss of your child. . . .

Nothing can prepare you for what it feels like to leave the hospital empty-handed, milk running, crying like you will never stop. Do not underestimate what is in store for you should you choose adoption. Perhaps the most important point is this: Never say "That won't be me." Don't assume you will feel any differently from the birthparents who have gone before you. Trust the women who are living it now to describe what it will be like for you.

Periodical Bibliography

The following articles have been selected to supplement the diverse views presented in this chapter.

Erwin A. Blackstone and Simon Hakim	"A Market Alternative to Child Adoption and Foster Care," *Cato Journal*, Winter 2003.
Susan Bordo	"Adoption," *Hypatia*, Winter 2005.
Doug Brunk	"How to Prepare for Adoption," *Internal Medicine News*, December 15, 2004.
Andrew Hale	"Why Weren't We Told?" *Community Care*, January 22, 2004.
Nancy Hanner	"Demystifying the Adoption Option," *Newsweek*, February 10, 2003.
Christina Odone	"Parenthood Is No Longer a Matter of Blood; It Has to Be Defined by State Regulation," *New Statesman (1996)*, November 11, 2002.
Marvin Olasky	"Another Big Media Miss," *Conservative Chronicle*, December 1, 2004.
Lisa Rauschart	"Not 'Unadoptable': New Effort to Find Homes for Older Foster Children," *World & I*, August 2004.
Bette Sack	"Do We Really Cherish Our Kids? Sentimental Media Messages Suggest One Thing, but the Reality Is Something Else," *Minneapolis–St. Paul Magazine*, December 2001.
Sarah Schafer	"Charity Begins at Home: The Middle Class Is Starting to Reach Out to Orphans," *Newsweek International*, July 25, 2005.
Michele G. Sullivan	"Adoption Not Tied to Increase in Risky Behavior Compared with Nonadopted," *Family Practice News*, July 1, 2004.

Whose Rights Should Be Protected in the Adoption Process?

Chapter Preface

How to balance the rights of biological parents, adoptive parents, and the child is an ongoing challenge in the adoption process. In the United States, adoption-rights debates have often focused on custody battles between the biological parents and the adoptive parents. A majority of states require a birth mother to wait at least one day after giving birth to give legal consent for adoption of her baby. Generally, this consent can be retracted within twenty-one days. However, if the biological father did not sign consent papers or was not informed of the adoption until after the fact, he may sue and win custody of the child even years after the adoption was finalized. Many of the high-profile custody battles of recent years have involved such conflicts between biological fathers and adoptive parents.

In an attempt to protect the rights of biological fathers as well as adoptive parents, Florida passed a law in 2002 that required women to disclose the name and address of the father of a baby offered for adoption. If the woman was unsure of the father's identity or whereabouts, she had to place notices in local newspapers describing any men who may have fathered her child. In the newspaper notice, the mother had to give her full name, describe herself, list descriptions of the possible father, and identify the likely date and location of the conception. These notices ran once a week for four weeks.

Many were appalled by Florida's law. Jeanne Tate, an adoption lawyer and executive vice president of the Florida Association of Adoption Professionals, found the notices "horrible and degrading." Likening the newspaper notices to a finger-pointing "scarlet letter," Tate represented a woman who wished to have her husband adopt her twelve-year-old son. Because the mother was married to a man who was not the father of her son, Tate explains, she had "to publish her sexual history from twelve years ago, where neighbors, friends, and other school parents [could] read all about it." Many adoption counselors, moreover, feared that the law would discourage adoptions and possibly drive more birth mothers to have abortions rather than face the embarrassment and humiliation of publishing their sexual histories.

Six women formally challenged Florida's adoption law, stating that it was an unconstitutional invasion of privacy. As a result, Palm Beach County judge Peter Blanc ruled that rape victims were exempt from the law, but he upheld the statute for other circumstances—including cases involving pregnant teenagers. Florida state representative Evelyn Lynn, who supported the law, claimed that it would make adoptions less vulnerable to after-the-fact challenges from birth parents. "We have been a state where people are afraid to adopt children," stated Lynn. "I don't see [the law] as punishing anyone," she explained. "I see it as protecting children."

In the end, an appellate court repealed Florida's adoption law. But the controversy it stirred illuminates the difficulties that are involved in ensuring that the rights of all parties are protected in the adoption process. The authors in the following chapter examine these concerns in greater detail.

> "[Adoption professionals use coercive methods] to guarantee the surrender of [a birth mother's] child."

The Rights of Birth Mothers Should Be Protected

Origins Canada

The authors of the following viewpoint maintain that adoption professionals, seeking to obtain babies for adoptive parents, often coerce birth mothers into giving up their infants for adoption. Social workers, counselors, and other professionals may tell the birth mother that she would be an unfit parent and discourage her friends and family members from offering support that might allow her to keep her baby. In addition, counselors may lie or withhold information from the birth mother—even taking the baby from the mother before she signs legal consent forms. Thus birth mothers are often denied their right to take as much time as they need to decide about adoption, the authors conclude. Origins Canada is a support group for people separated from family members by adoption.

As you read, consider the following questions:

1. According to Origins Canada, what might an adoption professional say to a mother to convince her that she is obligated to give up her baby?

2. How do adoption professionals keep a birth mother from bonding with her baby, in the authors' opinion?

3. According to the authors, what protections are provided to families by the 1948 Universal Declaration of Human Rights?

T he adoption "counselors" like to say "It's your choice", all the while making it seem as if you have no other real options. They have lots of training in "counseling" expectant mothers and grandparents-to-be so they can get more babies for customers. Do mothers (and fathers) really "choose" adoption?

Common Coercion Tactics

Below is a list of some common practices used systemically by the adoption industry on single mothers in English-speaking nations from about 1950 onwards, as means of obtaining babies for adoption. These tactics might variously have been applied by social workers, clergy, adoption "counselors", adoption "facilitators", nurses, nuns, clergy, doctors or others with a vested interest in obtaining a baby to broker for adoption.

A. Psychological Coercion. Purpose: To convince you that you were unfit as a mother and thus had to give your baby to people "more fit" or "more deserving."

Methods used by "Adoption Professionals":

1. You were told you that you were unfit to be a mother because you were "unwed."

2. You were told that you would be inadequate as a mother.

3. You were told that keeping your baby would be selfish.

4. You were forced to draw up a list comparing what you could give to your baby with what adopters could give.

5. It was stressed to you that your baby "needed a two-parent family."

6. It was stressed to you that the needs of your baby came before your own needs and that you could not fulfill your baby's needs.

7. The doctor who delivered your baby told you that you must sign-over your baby to him for adoption. (Did you later find out that the baby was adopted by friends of the doctor?)

8. You were told that if you did not surrender your baby, that your baby would be put into foster care until you did sign.

9. You are told that surrendering your baby is an expression of how much you love your baby (Message: if you keep your baby then you don't love your baby).

10. You are told that adoption is "thinking about what is best for your baby" (Message: adoption is best for your baby).

11. You are told that adoption is "putting your baby's needs first" (i.e., before your own needs. Message: your baby does not need you).

The Obligation to Surrender

B. Psychological Coercion. Purpose: To convince you that you have an emotional obligation to surrender your baby.

Methods used by "Adoption Professionals":

1. You were told to think only of the joy that you'd "give to a couple who could not have children of their own."

2. You were told that if you changed your mind, you would be disappointing a wonderful "mother" who was "waiting for her first baby."

3. You were told that you could not keep your baby as your baby has been promised to someone already.

4. You were encouraged to have the adopters pay your medical or living expenses such that you felt you "owed" them your baby.

5.You were encouraged to meet with the adopters and after meeting them felt you could not bear to disappoint them by choosing to keep your baby.

6. You were encouraged to establish a relationship with the adopters, and then "fell in love" with them prior to surrender.

7. You were told by your parents that you could come home once you had "disposed of the problem" (i.e., surrendered your baby).

8. You were encouraged to have the adopters in the labour or delivery room with you, for the birth of "their" baby, and thus you felt you could not bear to disappoint them by "changing your mind."

Blocking Personal Support

C. Psychological Coercion. Purpose: To remove from you all personal support systems and make you reliant on adoption professionals for advice, counselling and emotional support. To distance you from any person who might try to provide alternatives to surrender.

Methods used by "Adoption Professionals":

1. Your family members or boyfriend were discouraged by adoption professionals from helping you.

2. Your family members and/or boyfriend were prohibited from seeing you.

3. You were incarcerated by your parents in a maternity home or wage home where adoption was stressed as "the loving option" and/or "the only option."

4. Contact with your parents, boyfriend, fiance, etc. was restricted by the agency, maternity home, or social worker(s).

5. Your correspondence in or out of the maternity home or wage home was screened.

6. Telephone use was restricted in the maternity home or wage home.

7. Your boyfriend was lied to by adoption professionals that the baby was not his.

8. You were told that your parents were coercing you by encouraging you to keep your baby, that "they only want to be grandparents."

9. You were encouraged to distrust anyone who didn't support you surrendering your baby.

Distancing Mother and Baby

D. Psychological Coercion. Purpose: To psychologically and physically distance you from your baby in order to increase the probability that you would surrender. To ensure that surrender of your baby was seen by you as "inevitable."

Methods used by "Adoption Professionals":

1. Your baby was taken from you at birth by either medical professionals or prospective adopters.

2. Your access to your baby in the hospital was severely restricted by medical and/or nursing staff.

3. You were put into a ward other than the maternity ward for recovery, a distance away from your baby.

4. Your baby was immediately transferred without your consent to a different hospital.

5. While still pregnant you were labelled a "birthmother," to put you into the mind-set that your only role in the life of your child was to give birth.

6. You asked for your baby and were told "No!"

7. You were told that you were not allowed to see your baby unless/until you signed the surrender papers.

8. You asked for your baby and were told that it was best that you did not see your baby.

The "Horrible Birthmother"

Adoption laws are mostly written by men, who have no idea that motherhood is a great unknown until it actually happens. We frequently hear about the horrible birthmother who so inconsiderately changes her mind, as if a change of heart is a sin. Yes, the prospective parents will face real pain if the birthmother decides to keep her baby. But the cold truth is that no one is going to leave that hospital without pain. The potential birthmother is expected to bear the pain, and to bear it FOREVER. When she backs away from that pain, she is treated as if she has violated a contract, much as if she were selling a car, not relinquishing a child.

Heather Lowe, "A Birthmother's View of Adoption:
Suggestions for Reform," www.adopting.org/
BirthmothersViewOfAdoption.html, 1999.

9. You were given general anesthetic for the birth and kept under anesthetic until your baby was removed for adoption.

10. You were given mind-altering drugs such as scopalamine by medical staff for several days after the birth in order to induce amnesia.

11. Your signature was obtained while under the influence of mind-altering drugs administered to you by medical staff.

12. The drug Stilboestrol was administered to you as a lactation suppressant without your consent.

13. You asked for your baby back and the adopters stalled until the "revocation of consent" period had expired.

E. Psychological Coercion. Purpose: To psychologically trauma-tize you to decrease the chances of you bonding with your baby.

Methods used by "Adoption Professionals":

1. Information about labour and delivery was deliberately kept from you such that you were scared and trauma-tized by the unfamiliar process once labour began.

2. You were left isolated and alone during labour.

3. If there was a hospital attached to the maternity home, were you and other inmates forced to dispose of the placentas?

4. You were physically assaulted and/or mutilated by hospi-tal personnel during labour and/or birth.

5. You were called derogatory names or otherwise derided by doctors, nurses or medical personnel during your pregnancy, labour or birth.

6. The episiotomy was cut, or sewn-up, without anesthesia.

7. The episiotomy cut thru ligaments, was cut down your leg, or was otherwise unnecessarily large.

F. Financial Coercion. Purpose: To make you feel financially pressured to surrender. Note: young single mothers are often in a financially vulnerable situation anyway and thus financial coer-cion is often a major factor.

Methods used by "Adoption Professionals":

1. You are told, or led to believe, that no social assistance was available that would provide you with the financial support necessary to enable you to keep your baby.

2. You are told near or after the birth that if you change your mind, you would be liable for paying for medical bills or other costs beyond your ability to pay.

3. The hospital refused to release your baby to you unless you pay them a large sum of money beyond your ability to pay.

Lies and Misinformation

G. Fraud. Purpose: To guarantee the surrender of your child.

Methods used by "Adoption Professionals":

1. Your baby was taken immediately into foster care with no explanation and kept there with the location kept secret from you until the social worker could use "abandonment" as a basis for revoking your parental rights.

2. You were told at some point that the adoption was "final" and found out later that it wasn't.

3. You were told that your baby had died at birth and later found this was false. Note, this is known in the adoption industry as "rapid adoption." ALL single mothers who were told that their baby was stillborn and were not permitted to see the body should demand to see the certificate of death!

4. You were told that the adoption was "final" and found out later that it wasn't at that point in time.

5. You were told that there were no other alternatives (information about social assistance was withheld from you).

6. You were led to believe that a promise of open adoption was a legally-binding agreement and the adoption later closed.

7. You were told you would "get over it" and be able to return to your "normal life."

8. The documents were signed by someone else forging your signature without your knowledge or consent.

9. You were informed after signing a "pre-birth consent" that it would be held binding in a court-of-law.

   H. Withholding information from the mother. Purpose: To get you to surrender by withholding known information about risks or negative consequences.

Methods used by "Adoption Professionals":

1. Information withheld about the known lifelong implications, risks, and emotional consequences of surrender. . . .

2. Information withheld about options that would enable you to keep your baby (i.e., financial assistance, temporary foster care, foster care for you and your child together, temporary guardianship, or filing through court for child support from your baby's father).

3. Information withheld about your right to independent legal counsel to explain the legal document you were signing and the legal ramifications of it and to be present in the room to protect your rights as you signed it.

4. Information withheld about the existence of a "revocation of consent" period.

5. You were not permitted to read the documents you were signing.

6. You were not given a copy of the documents you signed.

7. You were pressured to decide on adoption while still pregnant, or to surrender your infant without being able to first care for your infant for several weeks postpartum in order to make an informed decision about motherhood.

8. Information withheld from you about your right to take as many days, weeks or months as you needed before deciding on adoption, if you decided on it at all.

9. Information withheld about your right to care for and nurture your baby in the hospital.

10. Information withheld about your right to take your baby home from the hospital with you.

A Mother's Rights

In Contrast: Your Rights as a Mother:

These are some of the rights that may have been denied to you, no matter what your age or social situation was when you gave birth:

- **You had the right** to see your baby after he/she was born.

- **You had the right** to hold, nurse, and care for your baby.

- **You had the right** to be told the sex of your baby.

- **You had the right** to independent legal counsel to explain the legal documents you were signing and to be present when you signed them.

- **You had the right** to care for your baby without feeling pressured to decide about adoption within ANY certain time period.

- **You had the right** to adequate financial support which would have enabled you to keep and raise your baby.

These rights come from application of the Universal Declaration of Human Rights, which has since 1948 guaranteed ALL citizens of Canada, the U.S. and other nations these protections:

- *Article 12*—No one shall be subjected to arbitrary interference with his privacy, FAMILY, home or correspondence, nor to attacks upon his honour and reputation. Everyone has the right to the protection of the law against such interference or attacks.

- *Article 16(3)*—The family is the natural and fundamental group unit of society and is entitled to protection by society and the State.

- *Article 25(1)*—Everyone has the right to a standard of living adequate for the health and well-being of himself and of his family, including food, clothing, housing and medical care and necessary social services, and the right to security in the event of unemployment, sickness, disability, widowhood, old age or other lack of livelihood in circumstances beyond his control. (2) Motherhood and childhood are entitled to special care and assistance. All children, whether born in or out of wedlock, shall enjoy the same social protection.

DECISION: The ability to make a fully-informed, non-coerced choice between two or more viable options. Starvation, homelessness, or harm to our children are NOT viable options.

No Legal Authority

How They Committed a Crime by Taking Our Babies.

Abduction is illegal in most civilized nations. Example: the *Criminal Code of Canada* states, "(281) Abduction of Person Under Fourteen—Every one who, **not being the parent**. . . unlawfully **takes**, entices away, **conceals, detains, receives or harbours** that person with intent to **deprive a parent**. . . **of the possession of that person** is guilty of an indictable offence and liable to imprisonment for a term not exceeding ten years."

They had no "legal authority" to take our children away from us any more than they would have had the legal authority to do it to an older, married mother. If your baby was taken and withheld from you *before* you signed any surrender papers, it was abduction.

"Good adoption practice ... [requires]
the gathering of the fullest possible information about the birth father and
for the safeguarding of his significance."

The Rights of Birth Fathers Should Be Protected

Gary Clapton

In the following viewpoint Gary Clapton discusses his study of thirty men whose children had been put up for adoption. Clapton discovered that a majority of these men opposed the adoption, felt distressed after it was finalized, and later wished to contact their surrendered child. Furthermore, the author notes, researchers and professionals involved in adoption often ignore or scorn birth fathers. Clapton maintains that birth fathers should have more representation in the adoption process—for the benefit of birth fathers who care about their children and for adopted children, who may later search for their natural parents. Clapton, a postadoption counselor, is the author of Birth Fathers and Their Adoption Experiences.

As you read, consider the following questions:

1. How many of the thirty birth fathers studied by Clapton wanted greater access to information about their child?

Gary Clapton, *Birth Fathers and Their Adoption Experiences,* London, UK: Jessica Kingsley Publishers, 2003. Copyright © 2003 Gary Clapton. Adapted from the original. Reproduced by permission of Jessica Kingsley Publishers.

2. In the author's opinion, what kind of gender role assumptions are often made in textbooks about adoption?

3. In what cases might a birth father's perspective be of value, in Clapton's view?

[M]y] study [of 30 men] has uncovered a depth and variety in the experiences and identities of men who are birth fathers and brought an understanding to their enduring feelings about their children. In summary, we have seen how at the time of the adoption, 25 teenage men felt that they had been in a steady relationship. An exploration of the various stages and associated changes in the men's lives showed the impact of becoming fathers, the adoption and the way that they had come to feel about their child. We saw how feelings of fatherhood emerged and grew for a majority of the group and how only one fits the stereotype of an irresponsible young man who abandons a pregnant girl friend. Over a half of the men in the study were against the adoption of their child and it has been shown that 21 out of the 30 men underwent considerable distress in the weeks and months after the adoption. Also we have seen how the negative feelings arising from the experience of adoption cast a long shadow in their subsequent lives and relationships. For instance, nine of the men had no other children. Their child was rarely far from their thoughts, with feelings of parenthood, loss and concern for the child featuring prominently. Most of them had sought or offered contact with their adult child and 20 out of 30 were in favour of greater access to information about the child. . . . Finally, it has been shown that the experiences of the birth fathers in this study have many similarities with those in studies of birth mothers. . . .

Adoption Policy and Guidance

This study has shown that some birth fathers had wished to be key parties in the overall adoption process from birth to any subsequent post-adoption contact, and were denied this opportunity. A UK [United Kingdom] High Court judge has called for an examination of local authority procedures to clarify the rights of birth fathers in adoption. Yet there is evidence that, as in the case of other areas of social welfare, views regarding the participation of men are mixed and knowledge of fathers may be based upon assumptions rather than fact.

[In 1965] when [E.] Anglim made a plea for birth fathers to be included in adoption practice with birth mothers, she raised the question of the profession's avoidance of birth fathers. In the same vein, [H.] Platts noted the existence of practitioner bias against birth fathers, as did others that followed. The accounts of the birth fathers in this study confirm that such bias existed in the UK throughout the period in question: the 1950s to the 1970s (with one man providing evidence of being marginalised in 1985). This is shown in their accounts of not being consulted or feeling unwanted—despite a willingness to be involved—and in some cases being actively excluded. Since the time of the men's adoption experiences it appears that little may have changed. [B.] Daniel and [J.] Taylor argue that a major text used in fostering and adoption practice repeats the gender role assumptions contained in traditional attachment theory by focusing upon mothers to the exclusion of fathers. They argue that such assumptions are not so much explicitly expressed, but are shown by the absence of any references to fathers in particular, and the use in case examples of only women's experiences.

Neglecting the Birth Father

A number of policy considerations flow from the discovery in this study that adoption happened to these men as well as to the birth mothers of the child. One is the manner in which birth parents are referred to in the official and professional literature. There has been a considerable increase in the US and the UK in the number of meetings and contacts between birth parents and their adopted children and research is underway

Harry's Story

Harry was prevented from seeing his child. Anger over this has remained with him since. At the time of the pregnancy he had been going with his girl friend for about a year. He was committed to fatherhood and looking forward to marrying and parenting. The baby's name was chosen by both of them. Two weeks before the birth—the birth mother was only 15, he was 19—the birth mother's mother intervened and plans were called off. . . .

Harry went to the hospital when he heard of the birth. There he found out that the birth mother was in labour. Despite being given permission to see her by staff, the birth mother's parents prevented this and there was a fracas and Harry left the building. Shortly after, a friend came out and told him the baby had been born. He did not see the baby then despite wanting to: "You feel very proud that you are a father."

The adoption went through. He held John for the first and last time three months later. This was for 30 minutes in the presence of a social worker. "It still makes me feel angry even thinking back on it."

Gary Clapton, Birth Fathers and Their Experiences, *2003.*

into these emerging relationships or has already been published. This has tended to focus upon the adopted person's experiences. Knowledge of the potential social, interpersonal and inter-familial dynamics of meetings between birth parents (birth mothers and birth fathers) and adopted people from the perspective of birth parents will be vital for post-adoption policy and practice which is presently informed only by a very small research base. In relation to birth parents, this research base is composed of birth mother experiences only. . . .

These omissions perpetuate the generalisation that adoptions only happen to women and recall the point made by Anglim regarding how professionals can contribute to 'a myth that suggests that a child born out of wedlock has only one natural parent'. There were only ten meetings and relationships between the birth fathers in this current study and their children, so all we have is a snapshot of these experiences and the men's views. However this study, with its findings from both contact and non-contact experiences and the revelation that there are 1500 birth fathers on ACRs [Adoption Contact Registers], suggests that any future literature should reflect this new knowledge of the existence and aspirations of birth fathers.

Hampering Contact Between Father and Child

A second policy matter lies with the UK Government and relates to the relatively low number of birth fathers who use post-adoption services: ACRs and support groups. This stands in contrast to the experiences of the men in this (albeit small) study which suggests that many more men than we imagine would benefit from post-adoption advice and counselling, if they knew how to access these services. The ACRs should especially be publicised and it should be possible to devise particular advertisements that appeal to birth fathers, ones that emphasise the value to an adopted person of knowing both their maternal and paternal origins. However, should birth fathers seek to register on the UK Government-sponsored ACR for England and Wales they face a particular problem. This is the requirement that they can prove that they are the birth father of the adopted child in question, either by having signed the birth certificate or being referred to as the father in the adoption proceedings. This study has shown that whilst some of the birth fathers could provide this type of proof, many would not be in a position to, as there was no requirement that they sign any of the adoption papers. Furthermore many of the men in the study were excluded from the events and so were unlikely to be mentioned in any of the various papers and documents.

This requirement of proof of fatherhood effectively excludes what may be thousands of birth fathers from registering on the second largest ACR in the UK and therefore prevents adopted people from achieving full knowledge of their origins. This is particularly disadvantageous in cases where the birth father is the only one who is willing to register; either the birth mother may be deceased or she may not be in a position to offer contact. This study's findings of birth fathers' long-held commitment to their children and what they can offer should inform a review of the above policy which effectively hampers contact between adopted people and their birth fathers.

Third, personal experience suggests that birth fathers remain to be involved or represented in all aspects of adoption policy and practice, e.g. adoption panels and training for prospective adoptive parents. The findings of this study of birth fathers—from their willingness to be participate in the adoption process, to their wish for contact, including evidence of considerable post-adoption distress—hopefully demonstrate the importance of not excluding birth fathers from adoptions. This inclusion would not only be in cases involving their children, but also where a birth father perspective might be of value, e.g. in training social workers.

Adoption Practice Both Pre- and Post-Placement

In the case of the men in this study, welfare and adoption workers clearly played decisive roles at the various junctures, perhaps not in the ultimate adoption decision, but without condemnatory attitudes the potential distress of the experience may have been minimised. A typical comment from the birth father was of not having had any choices laid out before them. An important consideration that emerges from these accounts is that, irrespective of whether an individual worker was seen as helpful, the sum effect of the attitudes of all welfare professionals, semi-professionals and others (secretaries, court officials), was felt to be hostile. Given the amount of distress experienced by the men in this study, adoption practitioners are advised to re-consider any assumptions that may be made about the relative 'strength' and coping skills of birth parents who actively participate in adoption plans. Attention to the needs of birth parents in the months after the adoption has rarely been the practice of adoption workers, concentrating as they have done on 'settling in' the child with its adoptive parents. The case for help in this phase for birth mothers has been accepted and, if the reports of the men are in any way indicative of the feelings of other birth fathers, then support ought to be extended to birth fathers too. This relates to the final point in this [viewpoint], concerning as it does the negative way in which birth fathers may be regarded and the attendant disadvantage to the child should this be the case.

A study of contemporary social work adoption case files has found an absence of information about birth fathers. The case of the birth father who won custody of his two-year-old daughter after discovering that she had been placed in foster care also shows that adoption practitioners may not regard the birth father as a resource, or his position as significant for the child. Others may not necessarily agree with this latter point of the long-term significance of the birth father. *The Irish Times* has reported on a case where a couple who were in the step-parent adoption process wanted to re-register the birth in order that the current partner be shown as the biological father. Their attitude was that 'the natural father was out of the frame, the child had an effective father so what was the big deal?' Good adoption practice pre-placement would seem to require the gathering of the fullest possible information about the birth father and for the safeguarding of his significance—for the benefit of the child who may seek knowledge of him in later life. The children of birth parents are best served when birth fathers are placed in the same theoretical position as birth mothers, thus officially acknowledging to the child its reality of dual parentage.

The birth fathers in this study have talked of emotions normally associated with social fatherhood without ever having patented the child in question. This suggests that fatherhood is more complex than we have hither understood it to be. It is now the task of Government, researchers and professionals (all of us) to act on what we know rather than what we think we know about fathers in general and birth fathers in particular.

> "*[There are] too many heart-wrenching stories of adoptive parents forcibly separated from their child years later.*"

The Rights of Adoptive Parents Should Be Protected

Jeff Jacoby

Rulings in adoption-related court cases place too much emphasis on biological parentage, argues Boston Globe *columnist Jeff Jacoby in the following viewpoint. When a biological parent changes his or her mind about surrendering a child for adoption, the child can be taken away from the only parents he or she has ever known, Jacoby points out. The legal system apparently believes that blood ties are more important than the devotion that adopted parents have to offer, he writes. This is an affront to parenthood and to adopted children, Jacoby concludes.*

As you read, consider the following questions:

1. Why has the author decided to pursue an international adoption rather than a domestic one?

2. According to Jacoby, why is Evan Scott being returned to his biological mother?

3. What will happen to Evan Scott as a result of being returned to his biological parents, in Jacoby's opinion?

F rom the moment my wife and I decided to adopt a child, we planned on an international adoption. Adopting a child from another country is more complicated, time-consuming, and expensive than a domestic adoption, but we didn't want to take any chances. We had heard too many heart-wrenching stories of adoptive parents forcibly separated from their child years later—not because they had done anything wrong, but because the biological mother had changed her mind, or the biological father had decided to assert his paternity, and an American court had elevated the claim of blood over the claim of love.

Families Torn Apart

It had happened in Illinois, when 4-year-old Danny Warburton ("Baby Richard") was pried, sobbing, from the only parents he had ever known and given to the stranger who happened to have sired him. It had happened in Michigan, when a screaming and terrified Jessica DeBoer was taken from her mother and father and sent to a couple in Iowa because judges had concluded that the biology involved in conceiving Jessica counted for more than the love and sacrifice involved in raising her. We wanted to be sure such a horror-show never happened to our adopted child.

The way it is happening now [in 2005], in Florida to Evan Parker Scott.

Evan was born in Jacksonville to Amanda Hopkins on May 5, 2001. On hand to witness the blessed event were Dawn and Gene Scott, the childless couple with whom Hopkins had agreed to place the baby for adoption. Two days later, the Scotts took Evan home. They have been his adoring parents ever since.

"We never really knew just how . . . blown away we would be by the love we feel for this very special child," Dawn Scott would later write. "We can't even describe it in words. . . . Evan completes us."

Kirk Anderson. Reproduced by permission.

Now that completed little family is being torn apart. By order of Florida Circuit Judge Waddell Wallace III, Evan is about to undergo something most small children experience only in nightmares—he is going to be sent away from his parents forever.

Evan's Story

At 3, of course, Evan is too young to be aware of the circumstances swirling around him. He has no idea that his biological mother was an unmarried 21-year-old who had moved to Jacksonville to get away from Stephen White Jr., the unstable 33-year-old who had impregnated her. He doesn't know that White "has a history of drug use and violent behavior," as Judge Wallace wrote in his Dec. 16, [2004], order, or that he was convicted of criminal assault for beating Amanda early in her pregnancy—a beating severe enough to send her to the hospital.

Evan has no idea that Hopkins willingly placed him with the Scotts for adoption because she knew they could give him a better life than she could. He doesn't understand that White was notified of the pending adoption before he was born, but waited months before taking the legal steps necessary to establish his paternity. He has no sense of the tortuous legal odyssey that ensued when a judge nonetheless allowed White to block the Scotts' adoption and demand custody for himself—an odyssey that has involved nine judges, endless trips to court, and a blizzard of motions, cross-motions, affidavits, and orders.

All this little boy really knows is that Dawn and Gene Scott are his mama and his daddy and always have been. They are his rock—the one true thing he has always known. Now Evan's rock is about to crumble.

The Scotts have been terminated as his guardians and removed as parties to the case. Hopkins, who freely placed Evan with them for adoption but now says she wants him back, is to have primary custody. The biological father—who never married the mother or supported her when she was pregnant, and who has a criminal history and what even the court calls "a temper that he has difficulty controlling"—is to enjoy liberal visitation rights. Soon ... Evan is to begin the transition from his home in Florida to the Illinois naval base where his birth mother now lives. Once he is in her custody, the Scotts don't know if they will ever see him again.

DNA Versus Parenting

This is what comes of attaching more importance to DNA than to years of devoted parenting. Only a legal system that believes ties of blood are the truest expression of parenthood could order a boy stripped of the parents who have raised and cherished him from birth. The universe as Evan Parker Scott has known it is about to implode. He is going to believe that his Mama and Daddy sent him away. What did he ever do to deserve that? And who among us would wish the confusion and heartbreak he will suffer on any child *we* loved?

| "Serving the best interests of children should be paramount in deciding all issues of adoption policy and practice."

The Rights of Adopted Children Should Be Protected

National Council for Adoption

The National Council for Adoption, an organization that promotes the interests of children through adoption, was founded in 1980. In the following viewpoint the council maintains that the rights of children are paramount in the adoption process. Thus, adoption policy should focus on finding the best parents for children in need—not on providing children to people wishing to adopt or maintaining connections to biological relatives, the authors contend. In addition, preference should be given to married couples when placing a child for adoption, although single parents may prove to be a viable option for some children.

As you read, consider the following questions:

1. Who are the "real" parents of adopted children, according to the council?

2. In the authors' opinion, what are some the biggest obstacles to adoptions that protect the child's interests?

3. In what cases may single-parent adoption be the best choice, according to the authors?

A *doption should serve the best interests of children.* The fundamental purpose of adoption is to serve the best interests of children. It does so by providing loving, responsible, and legally permanent parents when their biological parents cannot or will not parent them. Serving the best interests of children should be paramount in deciding all issues of adoption policy and practice.

A Loving Act

Making an adoption plan for a child is a loving act. Most birthmothers make an adoption plan based on their loving and responsible consideration of their children's best interests. They want their babies and children to have loving, stable families and homes, preferably with both a mother and father. Birthfathers, when they are involved in the adoption plan, are similarly motivated. Society should honor and respect birthparents, and especially birthmothers, for these loving, unselfish decisions.

Growing up adopted is healthy and normal. Adoption is healthy, satisfying, and good for adopted persons, not an enduring challenge to identity and wholeness. The adopted person may have additional questions and curiosities to sort out, but adoption is not a psychological burden or pathology as some theorists treat it. Adoption is the way one joined one's family, not a defining characteristic or lifelong process. Persons adopted as infants grow up as healthy and productive as people raised in their biological families. To the extent there can be a greater risk of emotional or behavioral problems for children adopted out of foster care at later ages, the correlation is not the result of being adopted, but rather of difficulties experienced prior to adoption, such as neglect or abuse. The vast majority of foster children make the transition into their adoptive families and grow up very successfully.

Encouraging Adoption

Ours is a society that glorifies reproduction, drives the infertile to pursue treatment at all costs, socializes them to think of adoption as a second-class form of parenting to be pursued only as a last resort, and regulates adoption in a way that makes it difficult, degrading, and expensive. We could instead encourage not only the infertile but the fertile to think of adoption as a normal way to build their families. We now ask young couples when they are going to have their first baby. We could ask them when they are thinking of expanding their family, and whether they are thinking about adoption or procreation or both. We could encourage all adult members of our society to think that their responsibility as members of the national community includes caring for the youngest members of that community when care is needed.

Elizabeth Bartholet, Nobody's Children, *1999.*

The Real Parents

Adoptive parents are the real parents. The "real" parents of the child who was adopted are the adoptive parents, because they are the ones who are legally and morally responsible for the child; they are the ones who parent. In general, law and society have appropriately treated adoptive parents the same as biological parents. In the best interests of children, we should continue to do so. The interests and well-being of adopted children are thoroughly intertwined with those of the adoptive family.

There is no right to adopt, only the right of the child to be adopted. The purpose of adoption is to provide the best possible parents for children, not to provide children for adults who desire to parent them. Adoption policy and practice guided by the best interests of the child recognizes no 'right to adopt,' only the right of the child to be adopted when his or her biological parents cannot or will not parent. Adult assertions of a right to adopt reveal a fundamental misunderstanding of the most basic principle of adoption: The whole purpose of adoption is to serve the best interests of children.

Children's interests, not ideologies, should come first. Some of the greatest obstacles to adoptions that would be in children's best interests are ideological. Some children grow too old in foster care because judges and social service workers insist on maintaining biological connections and pursuing family reunification, even when the household is harming the child and there is hardly a true family to preserve. Other children who could enjoy the benefits of family through transracial adoption instead remain in foster care because someone in authority believes the prospective parents have the wrong skin color.

Because some foreign authorities oppose the idea of Americans taking the mother country's children, many foreign children languish in orphanages instead of being adopted internationally—thus, sacrificing the children's well-being to national pride. The first, best choice for placing an orphaned child born in another country is an adoptive family within his or her country of origin. But for many children, this option is not available, and they are left to grow up in an orphanage, when they could have been part of a true family through international adoption.

Mother-and-Father Parenting

Consistent with the child's best interests, preference in adoption placements should be given to families that offer married mother-and-father parenting. Recent research has confirmed the teaching of centuries of historical experience that married mother-and-father parenting is most likely to produce the best outcomes for children. Because the goal of marriage is to be lifelong, married-couple parenting provides children greater security and permanence, and data show that adoptive parents divorce at lower rates than biological parents. Children also benefit from receiving both maternal and paternal love, which are complementary and distinct, and from having both male and female role models in their immediate family. For all these reasons, adoptive placements should be with husband-and-wife couples, whenever possible.

This principle is further substantiated by the fact that those who make adoptive placement decisions tend to choose married couples. Ensuring that their children have a married mother and father is one of the major reasons birthmothers give for making an adoption plan. Those who make placement decisions for foster children choose husband-and-wife couples two-thirds of the time and would do so at a higher percentage if there were more married couples seeking to adopt these children. There are 55-million married-couple households in America—471 for every child who is waiting to be adopted out of foster care. A major goal of child welfare policy should be the recruitment and preparation of many more of these couples to adopt the 116,653 children in foster care who had been freed for adoption as of September 30, 2002.

Adoption Alternatives

Single-parent adoption is in the best interests of some children. Children's alternatives for prospective adoptive parents vary significantly depending on diverse factors, such as the age of the child and any special needs the child may have. Children in foster care and foreign orphanages, who are older or have special needs, often have limited prospects for parents. Many children across America benefit greatly from loving, permanent relationships with single adoptive parents. Especially for some older children, single-parent adoption can be the best option available. But adoptive placements of healthy infants should generally be with husband-and-wife couples, because there are many such couples ready to adopt them. The question of who may adopt a particular child should be based on that child's best interests, given the alternatives that exist for that child.

Privacy Issues

Mutual consent should decide issues of privacy and openness. The right to maintain or waive one's privacy in adoption is essential to the human rights and personal dignity of adopted persons, birthparents, and adoptive parents. Adoption policy and practice should not empower one party to adoption to receive identifying information or unilaterally impose contacts without the consent of another party.

Search and reunion advocacy is commonplace in the media, but the range of views regarding privacy in adoption is actually as varied and personal as there are parties to adoption. In the context of the media's fascination with openness in adoption, it is important to remember that the many who prefer privacy cannot discuss their views publicly without sacrificing the very privacy they desire to protect. Birthparents and adult adopted persons who desire to have contact should be able to do so, when *both* agree. Otherwise, both should be able to control the release of their identifying information and whether and when contacts are to occur.

Research to date is inconclusive regarding the impact of openness in placements on adopted children, their families, and birthmothers. Some adoption advocates and practitioners question the wisdom of the exchange of identifying information and ongoing birthmother visits with the family. Others believe that fully open adoptions should be the norm. There is little controversy over such openness practices as: birthparent involvement in the selection of the adoptive parents; one or two meetings between birthmother and adoptive parents before and/or at placement; and letters and photographs for agreed-upon times following placement. In practice, birth-mothers and adoptive parents are working out agreements regarding degrees of placement openness; the substantial majority of agreements do not involve ongoing visits.

Periodical Bibliography

The following articles have been selected to supplement the diverse views presented in this chapter.

Yasmin Alibhai-Brown   "A Route to Stability," *Community Care*, April 17, 2003.

Community Care   "Behind the Headlines: Birth Parents," April 22, 2004.

Thomas Fields-Meyer   "Home Safe: New Laws Allow Women to Leave Newborns with Authorities . . . but Is Legal Abandonment a Good Thing?" *People Weekly*, March 17, 2003.

Barbara Howard   "Adoption and Its Challenges," *Pediatric News*, September 2005.

Nicholas Kristof   "Shaming Young Mothers," *New York Times*, August 23, 2002.

Liane Leshre   "Wrongful Adoptions, Fewer Secrets and Lies, but Agencies Fail at Full Disclosure," *Trial*, April 1999.

Celeste McGovern   "Tangled Web of Embryo Adoption," *Report*, March 31, 2003.

Peter Opper   "Preventing Heartbreak in Adoption: Understanding the Rights of All Parties," *American Journal of Family Law*, Fall 2005.

Katha Pollitt   "Slut Patrol," *Nation*, September 30, 2002.

Barbara White Stack   "Parental Rights," *IRE Journal*, May/June 2000.

Daniel Wise   "Teen Father's Rights Restored in Adoption," *New York Law Journal*, November 22, 1999.

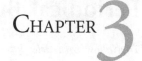

CHAPTER 3

What Types of Adoption Should Be Encouraged?

Chapter Preface

A wide variety of family forms exist in America today. Children may be raised by married, single, divorced, or step parents; some youths grow up in homes headed by grandfathers, aunts, foster parents, or guardians. In addition, a growing number of people are crossing racial boundaries when choosing spouses and when adopting children. Among these nontraditional families are nearly 10 million gays and lesbians who are raising up to 14 million children, according to the Lambda Legal Defense and Education Fund, a national gay rights organization. And increasingly, gays and lesbians are choosing adoption as a way to become parents.

While adoption by gay or lesbian individuals is legal in nearly every state, few states allow joint adoptions by same-sex couples. New Jersey was the first state to declare that neither sexual orientation nor marital status could be used against couples seeking to adopt. As this volume goes to press, New Jersey, as well as New York and California, have legalized second-parent adoption, in which a coparent can adopt the biological or adopted child of his or her nonmarital partner.

In recent years several professional organizations, including the Child Welfare League, the American Psychological Association, and the American Academy of Pediatrics, have published statements supporting adoption by gays and lesbian couples. These groups contend that sexual orientation has no bearing on a person's ability to be a good parent and that children of gays and lesbians are as healthy and well adjusted as children of heterosexuals. According to the American Psychological Association, some studies even suggest "that lesbian mothers' and gay fathers' parenting skills may be superior to those of . . . heterosexual parents." Adoption scholar and law professor Joan Hollinger agrees, noting that gay people may be more suited to adopt abused foster children because "people who themselves have had a difficult time being accepted . . . [often] have special insight." By granting gay couples—and not just individuals—the right to adopt, their children would enjoy the increased security and stability of having two legal parents, these advocates maintain.

Critics of gay and lesbian adoption often argue that its supporters seek out research studies that support their views and ignore any opposing data. According to research psychologist Paul Cameron, organizations such as the American Academy of Pediatrics (AAP) have never commented on comparative studies of children showing that those with homosexual parents experience higher levels of domestic violence, substance abuse, gender identity confusion, and molestation. In one study that Cameron conducted of 150 gay-parented children, the interviewees attributed 94 percent of their significantly difficult family problems to the homosexuality of their parents. In response to the AAP's support of gay adoption, Cameron maintains that "gay-rights activists have been particularly adept at manipulating research and reports to their own ends." Furthermore, he asserts, "For the next few years we will have to live with the repeated generalization that all studies prove homosexual parents are as good for children as heterosexual parents, and perhaps even better. What little literature exists on the subject proves no such thing."

Whether adoption by gays and lesbians should be encouraged is just one of the controversies examined in the following chapter. Authors also debate the efficacy of transracial, international, and embryo adoptions.

> *"Research has shown that the vast majority of children of color who were adopted by white families have thrived."*

Transracial Adoption Should Be Encouraged

Arlene Istar Lev

Children of color, who comprise the majority of children awaiting adoption, deserve permanent homes with families who are sensitive to cultural and racial issues, writes Arlene Istar Lev in the following viewpoint. Although people of color should be encouraged to adopt, transracial adoption should also be promoted for the sake of minority children who might otherwise grow up in foster homes or institutions. Parents who adopt children of a different racial background do face challenges, but such adoptions are largely successful, Lev concludes. Lev, a family therapist, is the author of How Queer: The Complete Lesbian and Gay Parenting Guide.

As you read, consider the following questions:

1. The author's family exists at the intersection of what three big social issues?

2. What was the effect of the Multiethnic Placement Act of 1994, according to Istar Lev?

3. How have various African American friends reacted when Istar Lev asked them for advice on raising her black sons?

Arlene Istar Lev, "Parenting in the Gray Area," *In the Family,* vol. 10, Summer 2004. Reproduced by permission of the author.

I am an adoptive parent to two boys. My older son, at 8 years old, stands near eye-level to me. In all fairness, I am barely 4 feet 10 inches tall, and my son's birth mom is 6 feet, 2 inches tall. All I know about his father is that he was "much taller." I often forget how tall my son is, until I see him playing with his friends. He looks years older than them, standing nearly a head taller than the children a grade above him. He is quickly growing into a tall black man. We have tried to raise him with strong, solid self-esteem. He knows he is handsome, and he is proud—a word so overused that I fear it has lost its power—of his African heritage and his kinky hair, flat nose and thick lips. We have never sheltered him from knowing about the harsher realities of the world. He is aware of racism and knows about slavery. He knows that white people have been cruel to black people. But as parents, we have also done what we can to protect him from being a target of racism—as much as that is possible. The world he lives in is filled with people of many colors and ethnicities, who respect and honor each other's traditions and cultures. He attends a school whose aim is to raise "multicultural citizens of the world." He has never (yet) experienced any major disadvantages simply because he is black, or at least none that I have been aware enough to recognize.

But at 8, store clerks have started to eye this tall black boy fondling the candy bars, and he is about to face some ugly truths about being black in our society. It breaks this mother's heart to tell him that the police will treat him differently than they will his friend Jake simply because he is dark-skinned. Although he's been raised to speak his mind ("You're not the boss of me!") the truth is that dressing appropriately and speaking politely in certain situations might one day be a matter of life and death for him. Teaching a black man-child safety skills in a racist world is a tall order for white parents.

White Lesbian Moms with Black Sons

When we adopted our second son, a biracial boy, we expected that our sons would "have each other" as black men growing up in a house with white moms. But our three-year old is barely a shade darker than his olive-colored momma. Everyone kept telling us he would darken, but it's pretty clear by now that his rosy cheeks, slightly tan skin, and Irish nose, are here to stay. Most people read him as white, except for older black women, who stop me in the grocery store, lean in and say, "He black, right?"

"Yep, he is," I assure them, and they pat me on the back, offering me both support and appreciation. I know they think that his father must he black (which is true), especially when we are standing next to his darker skinned brother. They, however, also assume that I am partnered with my children's father. I suspect their support and appreciation might ebb if they met the handsome light-skinned other parent, the one the kids call "Mommy."

It is a challenge raising strong black men in this world, and a particular challenge as white Jewish lesbians. It is an especially unique kind of challenge raising a strong black man, whom most people will assume is white. . . .

Although I live my life at an intersection of many communities, I find we are warmly welcomed almost everywhere we go. My family appears to be respected and appreciated. Nonetheless, I am aware of sub-text, and a sometimes underlying tenor of nervousness. My email box is filled with people sending me kudos and hurrahs for speaking out at the PTA meeting about the lack of attention to Black History Month, or my criticism of the barrage of white faces on all the flyers, worksheets and biblical images sent home from Hebrew school (the Hebrew tribe lived in the Middle East, not the Midwest!). My letter to the editor on the way the word "adoption" is used as a synonym for unwanted ("I always felt unwanted in my family; as if I was adopted"), receives accolades, and my reminder to the African drumming instructor that not all blacks find salvation in Jesus, are met with thoughtful appreciation and apologies. However, the bottom line is that if I don't speak up, these issues are not addressed, and some parts of my family, some aspect of my children's lives, some piece of our souls, is invisible once again.

An Intersection of Issues

LGBT [lesbian/gay/bisexual/transgender] transracial adoption exists at the intersection of three huge political and social issues. The first is queer parenting. In some venues, I have to defend and cite research to prove that LGBT people are good parents, that we do not molest our children and, despite their immersion experiences at Gay Pride Events with oversize drag queens in sequins and dykes on bikes in leather, we do not make them gay. Children seem to be growing up just fine in our queer homes, and even with all of our efforts to raise them with progressive values, they seem to want to watch the same crappy Disney movies and wear the same environmentally hazardous flashing sneakers.

The second issue at this intersection is adoption. Adoption is not exactly the same kind of front-page issue as LGBT parenting these days, except of course when something goes terribly wrong. Adoption is one of those awkward social issues that everyone knows something about, but few people know much about (including sometimes the very people impacted by it). Nearly 100 million Americans have adoption within their immediate families—that's 1 out of 3 families! Yet, I find that even within families formed by adoption, there is often much silence about the topic. Hardly anyone I meet is "opposed" to adoption, but there seems to be an unwritten message that talking too much about adoption will highlight the differences of adoptive families from families who were not formed by adoption, possibly making adoptees and their families feel bad. . . .

The third issue that intersects the life of my family makes the two previous ones seem easy. Highly contentious, and far too large to tackle in one small article is the issue of race and more importantly *racism*. What can I say, as a white woman, in one or two, or ten sentences to encapsulate the history of racism and the legacy of slavery in this country that would convey the relevance and weight of race on cross-racial family building? It is at the intersection of these three social and po-litically laden concepts—LGBT parenting, adoption, and race—where lies the landscape of transracial adoption.

A Controversial Subject

More and more LGBT people are choosing to become parents, and as social institutions change to allow us to parent, adop-tion becomes a increasingly popular choice for building our families. The majority of children available for adoption, due to the complexities of racism both domestically and interna-tionally, are children of color. Transracial adoption is a con-troversial issue that has been the subject of numerous public policy debates. Remember, we live in country where it was il-legal for people to marry across racial lines until 1967. Biracial families are still viewed with suspicion or seen as "exotic."

In 1972, the National Association of Black Social Workers issued a position paper opposing transracial adoption. It was based on a belief that black children raised in white homes would be robbed of their culture and communities. Certainly, the experience of some transracial adoptees has borne this out: many are angry and feel that their parents tried to white-wash their lives. However, research has shown that the vast majority of children of color who were adopted by white families have thrived. They have a strong sense of racial iden-tity as well as life-long bonds with their adoptive parents.

Sadly, because of restrictions on transracial adoption, many children were simply not adopted and instead spent their childhoods in foster care and group homes. In the early 1990s, policy changes were instituted that prohibited discriminatory practices in adoption and foster care placements. Since the passage of the Multiethnic Placement Act in 1994, agencies now cannot consider race, culture or ethnicity as a factor in decisions to delay or deny a foster or adoptive placement. Its proponents believe the policy to be critical in ensuring that the thousands of African American children in foster care waiting for adoptive families will finally find permanent homes and loving families. Opponents say that this detracts attention from the more pressing problems affecting children of color and their families and does not address the huge losses for black children raised in white communities. Both sides make good points, and so far the actual impact remains to be seen. The issue of the maintenance of a child's ethnic, racial and cultural heritage has yet to be fully addressed in public policy or adoption process..

What Children Deserve

All adoption is born of some wounding. First and foremost, all children deserve loving homes. We must look at what has caused this "overload" of children of color in foster care, including the racist social policies that have contributed to it. We must look carefully at issues of poverty that make children of color "available" for adoption, domestically and internationally, and we must do all we can to ensure that birth families find support to help keep their families together. When possible, children of color should be placed with extended family and programs must be developed to encourage people of color to be adoptive parents in larger numbers. This provides an excellent opportunity for lesbian and gay people of color to expand their families. However, no child should be without a home, and no child of color should be placed with a family who has not been sensitized to the complex issues of transracial adoption.

Eleanor Mill/NewsArtII. Reproduced by permission.

The Importance of Cultural Heritage

One of the criticisms of transracial families is that we can't teach our children how to be black. Jana Wolff, author of *Secret Thoughts of an Adoptive Mother*, says, "Becoming black is an inside job, . . . [my son's] evolution into a proud black man will occur largely outside the walls of our home . . . well beyond the reach of my loving white arms."

Racism is part of the daily experience of people of color in this country, and children of color must be raised to understand their cultural heritage and taught skills to combat the daily racism they will be forced to encounter. Most white people do not fully understand these issues; few white parents are prepared to teach these skills, and perhaps no white parent is truly capable of fulfilling this need.

Many white families assume that it is enough to love their adoptive children and raise them without prejudice, not realizing that it is an emotional handicap for children of color living in a racist society to lack a positive sense of their racial identity as well as skills to recognize and combat institutional racism. My own opinions on these issues as a social worker, a family therapist specializing in LGBT families, and a transracially adoptive mom change with the direction of the wind.

Race Does Matter

Black friends ask me, "What can white people offer these children? Can they offer to sing to them in their own language? Can they teach them about their heritage and the strength of their people? How can a white person teach a child of color how to survive?"

My response to them is, "Children deserve loving families. White people will not do it perfectly, but they can be taught about cultural diversity, they can learn about the child's heritage, they can learn to speak the child's birth language. It is not perfect, but it is far better than the alternatives."

And I want to believe this, I really do. Then I speak to white parents of black children and Asian children who blithely report, "Race doesn't matter. I'm raising my child to be an American. I'm raising my child to be color blind and to love all people as human beings." I am appalled and embarrassed for white adoptive parents everywhere. I know these albeit loving and well-intentioned white parents are failing their children of color. Their children risk growing up feeling separate from others who look like them, and separate from their families, who do not look like them or openly acknowledge what their different experience of the world is like. I know that the system has failed these children by not insisting that their white parents be educated about the impact of racism before placing the children in those families.

A Community Collaboration

It is true that my son needs to develop skills that I am poorly equipped to teach him. I am challenged to raise my black sons to survive in a racist world. I ask African American friends for their advice. Sometimes their judgement is harsh: "Don't use me to be a role model for your children. If you can't fix up his hair right then you shouldn't be raising him." And I sigh, and think (but don't always say), "Oh please don't make my child suffer for my weaknesses. Please be a role model for my child, help me to fix his hair, teach me what I need to know, even if it's not politically correct to do so. Bottom line is *he* needs *you*."

Some people of color understand this. I read an email yesterday from an old friend, a black transman who is living with a white female partner and parenting her four children. He said, "I think of you often as I raise three white males and one white female to be the best they can be. I feel this somewhat cosmic balance as you raise two black males to be the best they can be. I have learned through direct experience the incredible amount of healing that comes about through these acts and the families we create. I know, or at least hope and pray, they will carry forth to future generations and real change will occur."

Children of color being raised by white loving parents have a different relationship both to people of color and to white people. After all, it is my white hands that rock them to sleep, and my white face that comforts them when they wake from nightmares. Once a parent adopts a child of another race and ethnicity, the whole family is transformed. The child is not simply the one who is "different," but the whole family becomes multiracial and multiethnic. Raising children of color has to be a community collaboration, whether it is a fair burden for whites, for blacks or for the babies themselves. These children are a bridge and a healing between all our history.

| "People of African ancestry have distinct traits and characteristics that are important to raising healthy children of African ancestry."

Same-Race Adoption Should Be Encouraged

National Association of Black Social Workers

The National Association of Black Social Workers develops and sponsors projects that serve the interests of African American communities. In the following viewpoint the NABSW contends that policy makers should place a greater emphasis on placing African American children with black adoptive families or relatives than on seeking to place them with white families. When minority children are adopted by white parents, they are cut off from their own cultural heritage and from the opportunity to develop a healthy identity, the authors argue. More efforts should be made to preserve African American kinship networks and to recruit black families to adopt black children, they conclude.

As you read, consider the following questions:

1. What is the most consistent factor in determining when a child should be removed from his or her home, according to the NABSW?

2. What is the effect of removing African American infants from their home and community, according to the NABSW?

National Association of Black Social Workers, "Preserving Families of African Ancestry," www.nabsw.org, January 10, 2003. Reproduced by permission.

3. What is the Interethnic Placement Act of 1996, according to the authors? Why does the NABSW believe that it should be repealed?

T he initial policy statement on preserving families of African ancestry was approved at the National Association of Black Social Workers (NABSW) Fourth Annual Conference in 1972. Known for this statement for over three decades, the emphasis has not wavered. Many thought that the organization's position focused exclusively on transracial adoption. Yet, this was one component of the position statement, which instead emphasized the importance of and barriers to preserving families of African ancestry.

In 1994, a more expansive document, *Preserving African American Families*, reinforced the 1972 position statement by stressing the following:

1. "stopping unnecessary out-of-home placements;

2. reunification of children with parents;

3. placing children of African ancestry with relatives or unrelated families of the same race and culture for adoption;

4. addressing the barriers that prevent or discourage persons of African ancestry from adopting;

5. promoting culturally relevant agency practices; and,

6. emphasizing that transracial adoption of an African American child should only be considered after documented evidence of unsuccessful same race placements has been reviewed and supported by appropriate representatives of the African American community."

Factors Affecting Child Removal

According to the United States Department of Health and Human Services, as of September 2001 over 556,000 children are in foster care and over 40 percent of these children are of African ancestry. Children are more likely to be removed due to neglect than abuse. This suggests that child removal and class considerations, such as poverty, poor housing, and lack of access to health insurance, are key to understanding why some children are removed from the home and others are not.

While substance abuse is identified as a factor in many removals, race is the most consistent factor contributing to the decision to remove children and place them in foster care. When substance abuse is an authentic factor, the time line for sobriety and the availability of effective substance abuse programs is generally longer than the time line for reunification.

The Multiethnic Placement Act of 1994 (MEPA), the Interethnic Placement Act of 1996 (IEPA), and the Adoption and Safe Families Act of 1997 (ASFA) each have negative consequences for children, families, and communities of African ancestry. MEPA/IEPA requires that states recruit families from all communities, especially those that reflect the race and ethnicity of the majority of the children in state foster care. This is a welcomed and important requirement.

Therefore, the state or agency is required to engage in outreach efforts that are directed towards communities of color as long as White families who wish to become foster or adoptive parents are not excluded. The IEPA provision, however, not only condemns considerations of race, color, and national, origin and by extension, culture, in placement decisions; it also imposes financial sanctions for public and voluntary agencies that receive federal funding if they are found guilty of such action. ASFA goes further by requiring the filing of termination of parental rights within 15 of 22 months after a child enters out-of-home placement. Together, the legislation is contradictory and appears oblivious to the realities of an unwieldy child welfare system.

Family Preservation

The focus of NABSW's position on family preservation has centered on four basic premises:

- "advocating for the rights of families to keep and raise their children in a loving, safe, and supportive environment;

- advocating for the right of kinship to raise their relative child in a loving, safe, and supportive environment;

- advocating for fair and equitable treatment of families of African ancestry who wish to adopt;

- advocating for families of African ancestry to have equal rights and access to children of African ancestry that are free for adoption."

The Historical Context and Disparate Treatment

Understanding the historical experiences and their impact on a group of people is essential to developing relevant support services. People of African ancestry have distinct traits and characteristics that are important to raising healthy children of African ancestry. These experiences are typically absent from assessment models and practice decisions that affect the placement of children of African ancestry into foster care.

The disparate treatment of children of African ancestry is clearly demonstrated in the child welfare system. Three separate Department of Health and Human Services (DHHS) reports document that when controlling for income, people of African ancestry are no more likely to abuse or neglect their children than other racial groups. However, people of African ancestry are more likely to be reported for abuse and neglect and are more likely to experience out-of-home placements.

A recent study found that physicians are more likely to report parents of African ancestry for abuse or neglect than White parents even when the injuries are the same. Children of African ancestry are also more likely to receive additional tests and screenings in an effort to detect injury than their White counterparts even where the symptomatology is the same.

Once in the system, research documents that children of African ancestry receive less program support services and fewer visits from child welfare workers. They are less likely to receive the necessary referrals and follow-up services. When they do receive services, they tend to be substandard as compared to their White counterparts.

The disparate treatment of children of African ancestry has been validated in a number of critical studies. Thus, contrary to popular opinion, parents of African ancestry are no more likely to abuse or neglect their children but they are more likely to be investigated, have children removed from their home, and receive fewer services that are often found to be substandard.

Developmental Issues

The developmental context is critical to understanding just how devastating out-of-home placement is to children, in general, and children of African ancestry in particular. Additional studies have shown that infancy and toddler hood are the two stages where removal from the home and community is most harmful to a child. Yet, the increase in the foster care population has been among infants and toddlers. Infants of African ancestry, in particular, are more likely to be adopted than older children of African ancestry. The impact of being removed from the home at this critical stage delays development, contributes to the child's inability to bond, and promotes persistent fear within the child. Children, even infants, who have been separated from their birth families, grieve over the loss throughout their lives.

An additional developmental consideration is that of identity development. Children of African ancestry learn about their identity from within the home and community. Identity is critical to being able to negotiate the world, understand one's barriers and realities, and feeling good about self. Identity forms the basis of character development, pride, and belief in achievement.

Cultural Influences

Out-of-home placements generally remove a child from their home, school, and community. They have poorer educational outcomes, such as lower reading and math scores. Children in out-of-home placements can receive upwards of 3 or more placements. On the average, children spend 33 months in foster care placement, with 17 percent spending 5 years or more in placement. Children of African ancestry are more likely to receive multiple placements and are more likely to be placed in care for a longer period of time than other children.

The significance of culture in the life of a person is profound. [According to the NABSW] "Culture is the essence of being human. Culture is the bridge that links the present with the past and the past with the future. Culture provides a sense of historical continuity. It is a protective device structured to eliminate trial and error in the past and the future. Culture is second nature. It is a person's values, beliefs, learnings, practices, and understandings that are passed on. . . ." Children removed from their home, school, religious environment, physicians, friends, and families are disengaged from their cultural background. They are denied the opportunity for optimal development and functioning.

Recommendations

1. *Repeal IEPA and ASFA.* Both MEPA and IEPA stress that states recruit foster and adoptive families from all communities especially those communities from which the majority of the children in the foster care system originate. NABSW supports the recruitment provision as it was put there to ensure

Black Adoptive Families Are Available

The North American Council on Adoptable Children's 1991 study, "Barriers to Same Race Placement," found that African American–run adoption agencies successfully placed 94 percent of black children with black families. Organizations like the Association of Black Social Workers' Child Adoption, Detroit's Homes for Black Children, the nationwide One Church, One Child Program, and Los Angeles's Institute for Black Parents all show successful intraracial placements.

The Black Pulse Survey, conducted between 1981 and 1993 and published by the National Urban League, found three million African American households interested in adoption. The study's numbers suggested that, were even a tiny fraction of those families allowed to adopt, any argument about a preponderance of children in search of loving black homes would be effectively moot.

Samiya A. Bashir, ColorLines, *Winter 2002–2003.*

that people of African ancestry and other people of color would not be excluded. However, IEPA emphasizes that one cannot consider race, ethnicity, or *national* origin in placement decisions. These two statements often create confusion for child welfare workers as they seem contradictory. The *law* does not take into consideration the cultural differences of people of African ancestry and the experiences that they face daily due to the racial divide in America. Therefore, children are far too often cut off from their culture of origin and their African ancestry is deemed unimportant.

The implementation of time limits for termination of parental rights is unrealistic and can be harmful to children and their families. For example, a woman of African ancestry incarcerated in a District of Columbia jail informed her social worker that she found out that her parental rights were terminated when she saw her child being "advertised" for adoption on a local television broadcast. She had particular concerns because the maternal grandmother had never been approached with regards to the child. Children of African ancestry have been "auctioned" in local newspapers, advertised for adoption, while their mothers are unaware that their parental rights have been terminated. Some politicians would argue for tighter reporting mechanisms to ensure that parents have been consulted prior to termination of parental rights. This does not address the oppressive nature of the policy nor does it allow for human error and interpretation. The realty is that these time limits are oppressive, and can be harmful to children.

2. *Mandate culturally competent services from staffing requirements to revise procedural and policy manuals.* Not considering the cultural influence in selecting an appropriate setting for a child can be extremely harmful. . . .

Adoption Counseling and Referral Services have over two decade's experience of successfully recruiting and retaining foster end adoptive parents for hard-to-place children. People of African ancestry have been accused of not adopting their children. Yet, despite structural barriers and discrimination, they have adopted at greater rates than any other ethnic group. Holding agencies accountable for cultural competence throughout the child welfare process is necessary. Parents and children should be given adequate services to address their needs. Monies should be made available to enable agencies to develop or purchase services from community programs.

Monitoring Outcomes

3. *Mandate that country and local governments develop community boards to monitor child welfare agencies and outcomes.* We recommend that each local child welfare agency convene a group of community members, selected by community and

faith based groups, to examine disproportionality in the child welfare system. Communities *should* be consulted and assisted with solving issues that impact their families. The problem of disproportionality must be addressed at the *local* level, with supporting federal mandates.

State and local community boards should also be charged with examining the impact of class on removal rates. It is unethical to remove children from their homes due to poor housing or poverty, particularly if the parents are willing to do what is necessary to change the situation. Too many children are removed for neglect. This indicates an over reliance on removing children from the home, as opposed to addressing structural issues, such as poor housing, income inequity, and employment discrimination against people of African ancestry, in particular, and poor people, in general.

Providing Incentives

4. *Provide fiscal incentives to preserve families through community-based prevention initiatives and incentives for kinship care and reunification with birth families.* Reunification should be the first option for children when removal from the home is justified. Providing families with needed assistance and increasing community-based resources that are culturally competent can assist in preserving families. When reunification is not possible, then the second option should be kinship care. Some advocates say that there is insufficient information to support kinship care as an option. Yet, people of African ancestry have, historically utilized kinship care for over three hundred years in this country. Formal foster care however has been found to produce identity confusion, poor developmental outcomes, poor educational outcomes, poor health outcomes, poor employment outcomes, and connections with the juvenile and criminal justice systems later in life. Kinship care should be financially and structurally supported to meet the

cultural paradigm of people of African ancestry. One size does not fit all. . . .

5. *Enhance recruitment and retention efforts in communities of African ancestry.* Emphasis should be placed on continuing to hold institutions accountable for recruitment in communities of African ancestry and the places where children originate. Caseworkers should be mandated to obtain the names and addresses of family members, both in state and out of state, who may be placement resources under custody, guardianship or adoption if the children cannot be returned to birth parents. This information should be obtained from birth parents and the children when the case first comes into foster care. Relatives on both the father and mother's side of the family should be explored. The importance of families of African ancestry having equal access to become adoptive and foster parents should also be stressed.

A media plan, including brochures, television and radio public service announcements, should be developed to inform communities of African ancestry about the true condition of the child welfare system, updates on new laws, opportunities for foster care and adoption, and parents should be made aware that their parental rights cannot be terminated if services have not been provided to them by the agency under the current ASFA provision.

Mediation

6. *Retain the use of Concurrent Planning and Mediation.* Mediation services wherein all of the key players in the child's life (birth parents, extended family members, foster parents, godparents, etc.) come together to decide the best interests of the child should be mandated. The mediator should be a trained person who is NOT employed by the agency. Mediation empowers parents and has been successful in making the best placement plans for children.

Concurrent planning should also be mandated. This will help to focus the parents and the workers to expedite plans for the child. It is important that birth parents understand their rights and time lines established for having children returned. Concurrent planning should include the possibility of returning home, kinship guardianship, kinship adoption, kinship foster care, adoption by foster parents or other non-related persons. Open adoptions in which the birth parents have some connection to the child's life should also be explored.

Protecting Children

NABSW has a long history of promoting the preservation of families of African ancestry, singled out for its position on transracial adoption nearly thirty years ago, the organization has always maintained the importance of finding culturally grounded options for children of African ancestry before giving consideration to placing our children outside of the community. The Indian Child Welfare Act has emphasized, for close to thirty years, that Native American children be placed within their tribe or the Native American community before being considered for placement in other communities. The cornerstone of this legislation supports the notion of the importance of culture in the lives of Native American children. IEPA, and ASFA seem to deny the importance of culture in the lives of children of African ancestry.

We believe that children must be kept safe and protected. In addition, we support the rights of families to raise their children. It is our belief that until the inequity and discriminatory treatment of people of African ancestry is resolved, then the child welfare system will continue to treat our children and families disparately. Ultimately, this should be a social justice issue for all people. It is in our collective best interest to commit ourselves to ensuring the well being of our children and families.

| "International adoption is a life-saving form of care for children who do not otherwise have families."

International Adoption Should Be Supported

Debbie Spivack

In the following viewpoint Debbie Spivack contends that people who adopt children from other countries are providing loving families for those in need. In contrast to the media portrayal of international adoption as corrupt and cruel, adoption enables thousands of poor and orphaned children to grow up in a permanent family and to become healthy, productive members of society. Spivack maintains that the public, who often confuse international adoption with baby selling and child trafficking, need to be better informed about the benefits of this form of adoption. Spivack is the executive director of Reaching Out Thru International Adoption, an adoption advocacy organization.

As you read, consider the following questions:

1. According to Spivack, how many children from outside of the United States are adopted by Americans every year?

2. What are some of the reasons that people distrust international adoptions, according to the author?

Debbie Spivack, "Speak for the Children: Little Things Really Can Make a Difference," www.rainbowkids.com, June 1, 2005. Reproduced by permission of the author.

3. What is the purpose of adoption fees, in Spivack's view?

International adoption is a life-saving form of care for children who do not otherwise have families. Yet, professionals and families find ourselves increasingly on the defensive from an unwarranted amount of scrutiny and criticism, both abroad and in the United States. Mainstream prime-time television shows in the United States, domestic and foreign press, and foreign politicians bombard the public with stories of kidnapping, corruption, body part sales, and greed that make it appear to those with no personal experience in adoption that international adoption is somehow an evil institution run by thieves, sinners, and ingrates. While these stories do wonders for television ratings, newspaper sales and political careers, they have a devastating impact on children whose only chance for survival and success in life is through international adoption programs.

Country adoption programs are closing everyday due to disproportionately negative media, misinformation and ultimately tainted public perception of international adoption. The time has come for adoption professionals and adoptive families to put an end to the propoganda and use our collective power to correct public perception. Otherwise, international adoption could soon become extinct, dooming millions of children around the world to childhoods languishing in underfunded orphanages, or on the streets, with dim prospects for adulthood beyond drug dependency, crime and prison. The international adoption community has a responsibility to act, for the benefit of these children, and the sooner the better.

Making a Difference

There are over 20,000 children from foreign countries adopted by American families every year, and hundreds, if not thousands, of dedicated professionals who devote their lives to bringing these families together. And we all have family and friends who have become as invested in our children as we have. Altogether, we number in the millions, and are a grateful, proud and passionate bunch who recognize the true value of our contributions.

Many of us silently wonder where our children would be today had international adoption not allowed us to intervene in the lives of the children who we cherish. It frightens us to think about it, let alone speak about it out loud! Yet, we must, for there are millions of more children who face the prospect of no such opportunities because of a brewing firestorm of damaging negative misinformation.

Sharing our personal stories, and educating those around us, can have a massive impact on the fate of other children. This is because social change can behave in many ways like epidemics—spreading exponentially through a population by one small exposure originated from a singular source, or a small group. This concept is articulated best by Malcolm Gladwell in his relevant book called *The Tipping Point*:

"... It's that ideas and behavior and messages and products sometimes behave just like outbreaks of infectious disease. They are social epidemics.... Think, for a moment, about an epidemic of measles in a kindergarten class. One child brings in the virus. It spreads to every other child in the class in a matter of days. And then, within a week or so, it completely dies out and none of the children will ever get measles again. That's typical behavior for epidemics: they can blow up and then die out really quickly, and even the smallest change—like one child with a virus—can get them started. My argument is that it is also me way that change often happens in the rest of the world. Things can happen all at once, and little changes can make a huge difference.... As human beings, we always expect everyday change to happen slowly and steadily, and for there to be some relationship between cause and effect. And when there isn't—when

crime drops dramatically in New York for no apparent reason, or when a movie made on a shoestring budget ends up
making hundreds of millions of dollars—we're surprised.
I'm saying, don't be surprised. This is the way social epidemics work. . . ."

It is time to use our stories, knowledge, experience and
power to educate the world that international adoption is a
wonderful institution that warrants positive recognition—not
undue focus on scandal. As a group, we need to "tip" public
perception of international adoption where it belongs, a positive blessing rather than a series of negative scandals. . . .

Opportunities for Children

International adoption is the single best opportunity for children who do not otherwise have permanent families to grow
up to be happy, thriving, productive members of society and
to achieve their personal potential as human beings. The experts widely agree that institutionalization is harmful to
children's physical, intellectual and emotional development.
Even the most lavishly funded orphanages fail to offer the opportunities for nourishment and development that a permanent family offers. Statistics from countries like Russia are
plentiful, which demonstrate that children who grew up in institutions had increased rates of suicide, drug and alcohol
abuse, and criminal activity. No alternative, including, foster
care, offers the same opportunities for a child as having a forever family to offer unconditional love and the resources for
their child to achieve his or her personal potential.

Many of us may assume that these facts were universally
recognized. They are not, and it is important to reinforce the
notion that a child needs far more than a roof over his head
to grow and flourish in his life—children need families who
will love and nurture them—in order to grow into secure,
productive and happy adults.

Addressing Hostility Toward Adoption

We should also recognize that foreign perception towards international adoption is often hostile due to factors such as cultural differences, lack of knowledge and, ultimately, fear. We need to understand that fear so that we can respond to it productively. Consider the fact that the hostility towards adoption may be due to a cultural bias in favor of bloodlines, a lack of understanding of adoptive parents' motivations and goals, and ultimately distrust towards with whom they cannot identify. Many foreigners wonder why would someone from halfway around the world want to bring a child from another culture into their home. And they assume the motives are bad since they would not make the same decision for themselves and their own families.

Distrust of this nature plagues international adoption in almost every country and is best demonstrated by the inevitably-spread, never-validated rumor that international adoption is simply a guise for the buying and selling of body parts and organs. Yes, it's true—this rumor is alive and well in many civilized nations from around the world! Even the BBC World (regarded by many as "credible") "reported" the dreaded "body part/organ" rumor as fact in Baku, Azerbaijan in 2004. Investigations into these rumors have ensued in every country where adoptions occur, and have never resulted in a single finding of truth. Nevertheless, it continues to emerge and threaten opportunities for children to find homes through international adoption in almost every country where such adoption programs exist.

We need to humanize ourselves in foreign countries so that foreigners can see our families, relate to us, and, perhaps, better understand our honorable motives. And they must see the children whom they sent abroad for adoption, growing and thriving through pictures, stories, and videos. Humanizing ourselves and our families to the foreign public is the only chance we have to overcome the fears that are widely held and extraordinarily damaging.

The misinformed state that fees paid for adoption demonstrate that it is easy for rich Americans "buy and sell" people like commodities. Again—educate! Tell them first that the process is anything but "easy." Tell them that adoptive parents open themselves up to the highest degree of scrutiny by the American officials and foreign officials to ensure that they are fit parents. Tell them about the hours you spent gathering documents to share with these governments including tax returns, criminal background checks, child abuse clearances, employment and salary verification, just to name a few. And, of course, recount the numerous meetings you had with social workers, approval at the state level then the federal level, all before going through this all over again on the foreign side. The world should know that American families endure months or years and a great deal of effort to demonstrate that they are fit parents, and that their motives are to love and nurture a child for the rest of his or her life.

Fees Are Not for "Buying Children"

Foreigners also widely misunderstand the basis of fees for adoption. Tell them that any fees paid during the course of this process are not to "buy" a child. Rather, fees are for services to ensure the integrity of the process and keep corruption away. Every protection put in place to protect children corresponds to procedures in both domestic and foreign processing, and that these procedures are onerous and must be followed to the letter of the law. Doing it right demands the navigation of laws, procedures and challenges by intelligent, conscientious, and ethical individuals who choose to dedicate their time and attention to help find families for children despite their qualifications to work elsewhere. The focus should not be on the fact that fees are paid, but, rather, on transparency as to how the fees are spent and assurance that no fees were given to a birthmother to influence her decision in favor of making her child available for adoption.

Critics should also know that international adoption is a non-profit humanitarian mission. Tell them that American agencies working in this field arc primarily non-profit, government-licensed and subjected to accountability on a regular basis for our activities. Individuals working in this field have often given up lucrative careers in other industries to help these children. We are highly trained, exceedingly committed, and passionate about the work we do. We want nothing more than to find homes and families for children who do not otherwise have these benefits. There are millions of children in this world who need these things, and we do not need to engage in illicit activities to find them

[We] should also correct the misplaced characterization of orphaned children from foreign countries as "resources" to those countries that should not be "given away" to foreigners. This argument sounds nice on the surface ... "resources" certainly has a positive ring to it. But think about it—children left to languish in orphanages or to fend for themselves on the streets (sniffing glue to stop the hunger pangs) are not being developed or utilized in a way that could reasonably be shown to render them resources to their country (unless you count the insulting suggestion that they should be preserved to join their birth country's armed forces). In any event, this argument is misguided, as the rights of children to grow into healthy and happy adults should be a separate and important concern that outweighs political considerations, imperialism and national pride.

Adoption Is Not Child Trafficking

And, most importantly, do not let those around us continue to "confuse" the terms "child trafficking" with "international adoption." Many of those with a political agenda use the term interchangeably to suggest that somehow adoption is morally corrupt. The concepts are truly diametric opposites, and the distinction is worth making at every opportunity!

Explain the difference! Child trafficking involves people illegally, immorally and often violently removing children from their homes and placing them with people who intend to use them for illegal and morally corrupt commercial purposes such as slave labor or prostitution. In contrast, international [adoption] involves adoptive parents who have spent months going through invasive approval processes, additional months or years of waiting for a child, all in the hopes of having a child to love and care for during the duration of their life. They follow the legal process of their child's birth country, as well as their own, to ultimately give a child a home when no such opportunity exists in their own country.

Indeed, child trafficking is a very real threat to the well-being of all children and must be routed out at all costs. It also exploits the desperation of birth mothers to want to do what seems best for their children under difficult circumstances by going around the law and procedures to achieve an improper end. It is incumbent upon all of us to correct this "confusion" by reminding those around us that the former is a poison, while the latter is a blessing. Using the terms interchangeably perpetuates the notion that international adoption is inherently corrupt.

Tipping the Public Perception

Finally, give them facts and resources. We have in our midst some fantastic legal and medical experts with credentials that are beyond reproach. Point to their extensive research, first-hand experience and praiseworthy articles when discussing your confidence and pride in the adoption system. Any critic will have a hard time refuting the impressive mountain of study behind your comments. Utilize these resources, and allow uninformed critics to challenge them!. . .

The Right of Every Child

It is the fundamental right of every child to have a family. The preferred priority for every child is to be raised by the families who give birth to them and vigorous effort should be undertaken to make that possible. Unfortunately, in many developing countries where "turning cradles" and orphanages are the social safety net for orphaned children this is not their reality. The routine practice of abandonment eliminates the preferred priority of staying with, or being reunited with a child's birth family. For them, the next priority should be to find a suitable adoptive family in the child's birth country. When that is not a viable option, and too often it is not, it is tragic for these children to spend their developing years languishing in institutions when there are families in other countries who would love and care for them as their own.

Susan Soon-Keum Cox,
"The Issues in International Adoption,"
Holt International Children's Services, www.holtintl.org.

It is time for us to "tip" the public perception of international adoption toward the positive. To accomplish this, we must first shift our perceptions of ourselves from lucky and fulfilled adoptive families and professionals, to advocates—voices for the children who have not yet been afforded that chance. We are messengers, presented with opportunities at every turn. We must start to take advantage. Little things certainly can make a big difference.

> *"Intercountry adoption is nothing else but an irresponsible social experiment of gigantic measures, from the beginning to the end."*

International Adoption Is Harmful

Tobias Hubinette

International adoption is an unequal and exploitive exchange between wealthy and poor nations, writes Tobias Hubinette in the following viewpoint. Furthermore, he notes, many children who have been adopted by parents of a different culture grow up feeling alienated from their own ethnic background. Most significantly, research reveals that international adoptees have higher rates of behavioral, emotional, and mental health problems than do nonadoptees. Hubinette (Asian name Lee Sam-dol) is a Korean who was adopted by a Swedish family. He was a graduate student in Korean studies at Stockholm University in Sweden when he wrote this viewpoint.

As you read, consider the following questions:

1. Who were the first Korean adoptees, according to Hubinette?

2. Which countries supply the most children for international adoption, according to the author?

Tobias Hubinette, "A Critique of Intercountry Adoption," www.transracialabductees.org, 2003. Reproduced by permission.

3. The suicide rate for intercountry adoptees is comparable to the suicide rate for what other group of people, according to Hubinette?

What is fundamentally wrong with intercountry adoption is that white Westerners adopt children, while non-whites in non-Western countries relinquish and supply those children. Intercountry adoption is in other words a one-way traffic and not an equal exchange of children in need between countries. Since its beginning after World War II when the supply of working-class children for domestic adoption started to run short, intercountry adoption has been the last resort to have a child for infertile couples belonging to the elite who feel a strong social pressure to fulfill the standard of the nuclear family. Intercountry adoption is widely perceived as a progressive and anti-racist act of rescuing a non-white child from the miseries of the Third World, something which legitimizes the practice in the first place. Besides, the bizarre situation is loaded with demands of loyalty, guilt and gratefulness as the wealthiest of the rich in the receiving countries adopt the most shunned and unwanted in the Third World.

Historical Prerequisites

Before World War II, no Westerner thought about adopting a non-white child. Racism was the order of the day of the colonial world order in a time when the West ruled the world. Before the war, different humanitarian organizations actually tried to place Jewish refugee children from Central Europe as a part of the Kindertransport into Swedish homes. Today we can read about the difficulties in placing those children through letters preserved at the National Archive of Sweden: "We don't want Jewish children. Aren't there any Aryan children?"

How could Westerners be prepared to adopt "non-Aryan" children from Korea already at the beginning of the 1950s? The answers are the Holocaust and de-colonization. The scope of the Holocaust created such a shock that the West was forced to change its worldview. The West realized that the Holocaust couldn't just be a German deed, and that instead all Western countries were "guilty" after 2,000 years of Anti-Semitism. The West went from open racism to the idea of equality for all races, at least theoretically. This idea destroyed the world order having dominated the last 500 years: that the West had the right to conquer, exterminate and rule over non-white people. De-colonization was followed by violent conflicts, and the first intercountry adoptees soon started to arrive.

The Korean and Swedish cases

The Korean War was not just a Korean war. It was a cynical and dirty war between the super powers that happened to take place on the Korean peninsula as two Korean states were dominated by two Western powers as pawns in the game. 3.5 million Koreans were killed on both sides representing over 10 percent of the population. The Korean War is considered one of the bloodiest in history considering the limitation in time and in geography, and the losses correspond to one fifth of the global war casualties since World War II.

During the years of war, soldiers from the UN-army started to adopt children. The UN-army contained most of the countries which would adopt the majority of the Korean children: Australia, Canada, Luxemburg, United States, Belgium, the Netherlands, France, Sweden, Norway and Denmark. Witnesses describe the Korean War as something close to genocide. The UN-soldiers killed tens of thousands of Koreans on both sides indiscriminately, and it is also important to bear in mind that almost all of the first Korean adoptees were products of unequal relations between UN-soldiers and Korean women.

The same pattern followed in other countries. De-colonized countries like India and Ethiopia became supplying countries as a consequence of international aid efforts. Especially in East Asia, dominating intercountry adoption as a region, the Korean situation became the standard. Wars and catastrophes in countries like Vietnam and Thailand resulted in intercountry adoption from those countries. Worth noting is also that many leading supplying countries in the field of intercountry adoption fall under America's sphere of influence or have been subjected to American warfare: Korea, Vietnam, Thailand and the Philippines in Asia, and Colombia, Chile and Guatemala in South America.

Sweden played an important role everywhere. The result is that Sweden has brought in the largest number of adoptees among all Western countries in relation to the native population: almost 45,000 from 130 different countries. After a pro-Nazi war history and a long tradition of race thinking, self-righteous Sweden after 1945 wanted to be the paradise for human rights, democracy and anti-racism. Another less idealistic motive worth mentioning was the sudden disappearance of adoptable Swedish children during the decade as a result of rapid economic growth and a high participation of women in the labor force, as well as the development of an advanced social welfare system. Even more important is Sweden's self image as the world's most democratic country, a self-image recently challenged by the sudden appearance of a vigorous National Socialist movement and racism towards non-Western immigrants including adoptees. Intercountry adoption is in Sweden nothing else but a national project to uphold the country's self-image.

Creating Social Problems

For countries like Korea, the almost insatiable demand for children has created huge social problems. Intercountry adoption has destroyed all attempts to develop an internal social welfare system, and the position of the Korean woman has remained unchanged. The Swedes have been forced to accept unwed mothers for a long time, but in Korea the children born out-of-wedlock instead disappeared abroad. In the 1970s, during the golden days of Korean adoption when Korean children like pets and mascots became status symbols among progressive whites, the pressure was enormous on Korea to find adoptable children. Temporarily relinquished children at institutions and those who simply got lost from their parents on the streets disappeared forever from the country. Intercountry adoption was also linked to the amount of money Western organizations gave to the institutions: as more children delivered, as more money received.

The consequences of intercountry adoption for supplying countries in terms of a national trauma and destroyed lives for the biological parents are today obvious in a country like Korea, the country in the world which has sent away the largest number of children: more than 150,000 in 15 Western countries. Interestingly, Swedish documentaries on intercountry adoption are always focusing on the "positive" side, while the equivalents in Korea always focus on "negative" aspects.

"In the Best Interest of the Child"

The expression "in the best interest of the child" is used as a mantra by intercountry adoption proponents. It is a fact that intercountry adoption has always worked for the interests of adoptive parents and receiving countries, never for the interests of adopted children or supplying countries. If it would have been "in the best interest of the child", then siblings would never have been separated, and every adoptive parent would have been forced to travel to the supplying country and pick up the child and at least tried to learn something of the child's language and culture. . . .

Adoptive parents have the right to choose between age, country, race, handicap et cetera. The fact that some countries have been favorites for adoptive parents says a lot about how much race thinking still continue to live on under the anti-

Mueller. Reproduced by permission.

racist surface. Korea in Asia, Ethiopia in Africa and Colombia in Latin America are countries whose children more easily can pass as whites compared to other countries in the same regions. Compare children from Korea to children from Malaysia, children from Ethiopia to children from Nigeria and children from Colombia to children from Bolivia. Furthermore, Swedish adoptive parents seem to have a clear preference for girls and "racially pure" children. Non-white girls are probably less threatening, especially for infertile men, and the last preference is nothing else but racism.

A paternalistic and neo-colonial thinking consider us adoptees to be eternal children. We are forced into an identity as adopted children, not as adults. At the same time we are the children of the whole Swedish society more than any immigrant ever can be. And first and foremost we are Swedes, we are not allowed to explore our ethnic origin. In spite of this total lack of respect and integrity towards the adopted child, the adoptive family continues to act "mother, father and child" even if this social anomaly never will develop into a biological relationship. Is it a right to have children? Is it a right to take others' children? Only a privileged white middle-class person answers yes on these questions. . . .

Outcomes of Intercountry Adoption

Studies on adoptees have been conducted ever since the first children arrived in their host countries in the 1950s, and the majority have been qualitative works based on small groups of children or adolescents with adoptive parents as informants and focusing on issues of attachment, adjustment and self-esteem. In the leading adopting regions of North America, Scandinavia and Western Europe, the field is heavily dominated by researchers who are either adoptive parents themselves or affiliated to adoption agencies. As a result of these obvious limitations, the outcomes of studies are almost without exceptions interpreted as positive, and problems that have been identified are attributed to a combination of pre-adoption and genetic factors as it is understood that there are no difficulties at all of being racially different in a white environment. As a consequence, there are few studies on adult adoptees and few quantitative population studies, while the politically sensitive issues of race and ethnicity are mostly dealt with in a shallow way.

However, recently new research have come to light, based on thousands of adult intercountry adoptees in Sweden due to unique possibilities in the country of conducting quantitative register studies, showing a less positive picture of intercountry adoption. Antecedents to the Swedish studies were conducted in the Netherlands already in the 1990s showing high frequencies of behavior and emotional problems among adolescent intercountry adoptees compared to equivalent non-adopted control groups. The new Swedish studies, by far the most extensive ever conducted on intercountry adoptees in any Western country up to date, clearly indicate that intercountry adoption is not as unproblematic and idyllic as it generally is conceived as. Instead the Swedish studies should be seen as the most scientific way of assessing the outcomes of intercountry adoption.

The adult intercountry adoptees were checked up in population registers and compared to equivalent control groups among ethnic Swedes. The results show that the group has substantial problems to establish themselves socio-economically in terms of level of education, labor market achievement and creating a family in spite of having been adopted to couples predominantly belonging to the Swedish elite. It is estimated that 90 percent of the adoptive parents belong to the upper and middle classes. In spite of this, 6.6 percent of the intercountry adoptees had a post-secondary education of three years or more compared to 20 percent among biological children of the adoptive parents whom they grew up with as siblings. 60.2 percent of the intercountry adoptees were employed compared to 77.1 percent among ethnic Swedes, and half of the former group belong to the lowest income category compared 28.6 percent for the latter. 29.2 percent of the intercountry adoptees were either married or co-habitants compared to 56.2 percent of the majority population. Intercountry adoptees have less often children, and those who are parents are more often living without their children if they are males or as single parents if they are females, thus sadly mimicking their biological parents' behavior. Males have more often than females indicators of social maladjustment.

Shocking Findings

Moreover, epidemiological studies show high levels of psychiatric illness, addiction, criminality and suicide compared to the control groups. The odds ratio for psychiatric hospital care was found to be 3.2, for treatment for alcohol abuse 2.6 and for drug abuse 5.2. The odds ratio for severe criminality leading to imprisonment stood at 2.6 and for suicide attempt 3.6. Females have more often than males indicators of poor mental health. The most shocking finding is a record high odds ratio of 5.0 for suicide compared to ethnic Swedes, in an international perspective only comparable to the staggering suicide rates registered among indigenous people in North America and Oceania, which makes parallels to cultural genocide ghastly topical.

In this perspective, it becomes more evident than ever that intercountry adoption is nothing else but an irresponsible social experiment of gigantic measures, from the beginning to the end.

> *"Children with parents who are homosexual can have the same advantages and the same expectations for health, adjustment, and development as can children whose parents are heterosexual."*

Homosexuals Should Have the Right to Adopt

Part I: Adam Pertman; Part II: American Academy of Pediatrics

The authors of the following two-part viewpoint maintain that gays and lesbians should have the right to adopt children. In Part I Adam Pertman points out that children raised by gay parents are as healthy and well adjusted as children raised by heterosexual parents. In Part II the American Academy of Pediatrics (AAP) states that children who have been adopted by one member of a same-sex couple should also be able to be adopted by the other member of the couple. Thus, children adopted by homosexuals could grow up with the stability of having two legally recognized parents, the authors explain. Pertman is the author of the book Adoption Nation. *The AAP is an organization of sixty thousand pediatricians committed to the well-being of children and young adults.*

Part I: Adam Pertman, "Adoption Wears Many Faces," *Los Angeles Times*, February 19, 2002, p. B11. Reproduced by permission of the author. Part II: American Academy of Pediatrics, "Coparent or Second-Parent Adoption by Same-Sex Parents," *Pediatrics,* vol. 109, February 2002, p. 339-340. Copyright © American Academy of Pediatrics. Reproduced by permission.

As you read, consider the following questions:

1. In Pertman's opinion, why are the courtroom arguments against adoption by gays and lesbians disingenuous?

2. What are second-parent adoptions, according to Pertman?

3. According to the AAP, what rights would children enjoy under legalized co-parent adoption?

Part I

T he common thread among all the states that prohibit or impede adoption by gays and lesbians is their stated desire to provide the best possible homes for children.

It is not homophobia, they assert, to enact laws and policies acknowledging the benefits of parenting by both a mother and a father who are married to each other. They invariably add—during legislative or courtroom debates if not in statutory language—that preventing homosexuals from adopting effectively protects children from being negatively influenced or even physically harmed by the adults who are supposed to protect them.

Ill-Informed Arguments

All those arguments are ill-informed and disingenuous nonsense.

If politicians and judges in these states truly believed their own words, they would act immediately to remove millions of supposedly at-risk children from families in which one or both parents are gay. More urgently, they would be using the legal system to attack the scourge of single parenthood—which deprives far more kids of two married, cohabitating, heterosexual parents than any other cultural phenomenon in history.

A serious effort to achieve either of those goals won't be mounted anywhere, of course, though some social conservatives probably would like to see it happen. But it won't for two principal reasons: Whatever their personal or political views, policymakers generally understand that there's little they can do to alter the reality that diverse families of all sorts are becoming commonplace in our country; and, more pointedly, there is no credible evidence that children raised in nontraditional families suffer from a lack of love, stability or safety.

Second-Parent Adoption

Both those points were underscored in a big way [in February 2002] when the American Academy of Pediatrics announced its backing for gays and lesbians in so-called second-parent adoptions, the mechanism by which one partner becomes a second legal parent to the other's biological or adopted children. Such adoptions have taken place in about two dozen states, although only seven and the District of Columbia explicitly permit the procedure. A few prohibit it or make it bureaucratically impossible; and one, New Jersey, allows homosexuals to adopt as couples at the same time.

The academy's support for second-parent adoptions is important not only because it puts the imprimatur of a highly regarded, mainstream organization on a controversial practice but also because an academy committee reviewed 20 years of research and concluded that children raised by homosexuals are just as well-adjusted as their counterparts reared by heterosexuals.

This is obviously good news for gay-rights proponents, as well as for advocates of nontraditional families. It would be a huge mistake, however, for policymakers to interpret the academy's findings too narrowly: The findings also should broaden the pool of prospective parents for the tens of thousands of children who live in foster care. There isn't a state that has enough applicants to give these kids homes, yet too many still prevent gays and lesbians from adopting.

It always has been tough to figure how anyone could conclude that a child was better off in his or her fifth foster home than in a loving, albeit untraditional family. Now, in light of the academy's findings, it's going to get even harder to view such policies as anything other than overtly homophobic.

The Situation in Florida

The situation in Florida, the only state to ban all gay and lesbian adoptions outright, shows how silly and counterproductive the debate has been. In affirming a state law forbidding adoption by homosexuals [in 2001], a federal court in Florida said that the three HIV-infected children being raised by a gay man (who had been named Foster Father of the Year) would be better off in a home with two married, heterosexual parents.

Never mind that children like these, with serious special needs, are languishing in every state without parents of any type. And never mind the convoluted logic that leads Florida to allow gays and lesbians to serve as foster parents but not to adopt the children they are raising anyway.

I just hope politicians and policymakers do keep this in mind as they consider the implications of the academy's findings: As a result of changes in federal laws, Americans can adopt in any state, not just the one in which they live. So the states that try to prevent or restrict a gay lesbian from becoming a parent cannot achieve their aim; they can only prevent children in their custody from getting permanent families.

Part II

Children who are born to or adopted by 1 member of a same-sex couple deserve the security of 2 legally recognized parents. Therefore, the American Academy of Pediatrics supports legislative and legal efforts to provide the possibility of adoption of the child by the second parent or coparent in these families.

Children of Lesbian and Gay Parents

Research suggests that sexual identities (including gender identity, gender-role behavior, and sexual orientation) develop in much the same ways among children of lesbian mothers as they do among children of heterosexual parents. Studies of other aspects of personal development (including personality, self-concept, and conduct) similarly reveal few differences between children of lesbian mothers and children of heterosexual parents. . . . Evidence also suggests that children of lesbian and gay parents have normal social relationships with peers and adults. The picture that emerges from research is one of general engagement in social life with peers, parents, family members, and friends. Fears about children of lesbian or gay parents being sexually abused by adults, ostracized by peers, or isolated in single-sex lesbian or gay communities have received no scientific support.

American Psychological Association,
"Sexual Orientation, Parents, and Children,"
www.apa.org, July 2004.

Children deserve to know that their relationships with both of their parents are stable and legally recognized. This applies to all children, whether their parents are of the same or opposite sex. The American Academy of Pediatrics recognizes that a considerable body of professional literature provides evidence that children with parents who are homosexual can have the same advantages and the same expectations for health, adjustment, and development as can children whose parents are heterosexual. When 2 adults participate in parenting a child, they and the child deserve the serenity that comes with legal recognition.

Legal Status for Coparents

Children born or adopted into families headed by partners who are of the same sex usually have only 1 biologic or adoptive legal parent. The other partner in a parental role is called the "coparent" or "second parent." Because these families and children need the permanence and security that are provided by having 2 fully sanctioned and legally defined parents, the Academy supports the legal adoption of children by coparents or second parents. Denying legal parent status through adoption to coparents or second parents prevents these children from enjoying the psychologic and legal security that comes from having 2 willing, capable, and loving parents.

Several states have considered or enacted legislation sanctioning second-parent adoption by partners of the same sex. In addition, legislative initiatives assuring legal status equivalent to marriage for gay and lesbian partners, such as the law approving civil unions in Vermont, can also attend to providing security and permanence for the children of those partnerships.

Many states have not yet considered legislative actions to ensure the security of children whose parents are gay or lesbian. Rather, adoption has been decided by probate or family courts on a case-by-case basis. Case precedent is limited. It is important that a broad ethical mandate exist nationally that will guide the courts in providing necessary protection for children through coparent adoption.

What Coparent Adoption Accomplishes

Coparent or second-parent adoption protects the child's right to maintain continuing relationships with both parents. The legal sanction provided by coparent adoption accomplishes the following:

1. Guarantees that the second parent's custody rights and responsibilities will be protected if the first parent were

to die or become incapacitated. Moreover, second-parent adoption protects the child's legal right of relationships with both parents. In the absence of coparent adoption, members of the family of the legal parent, should he or she become incapacitated, might successfully challenge the surviving coparent's rights to continue to parent the child, thus causing the child to lose both parents.

2. Protects the second parent's rights to custody and visitation if the couple separates. Likewise, the child's right to maintain relationships with both parents after separation, viewed as important to a positive outcome in separation or divorce of heterosexual parents, would be protected for families with gay or lesbian parents.

3. Establishes the requirement for child support from both parents in the event of the parents' separation.

4. Ensures the child's eligibility for health benefits from both parents.

5. Provides legal grounds for either parent to provide consent for medical care and to make education, health care, and other important decisions on behalf of the child.

6. Creates the basis for financial security for children in the event of the death of either parent by ensuring eligibility to all appropriate entitlements, such as Social Security survivors benefits.

What Pediatricians Should Do

On the basis of the acknowledged desirability that children have and maintain a continuing relationship with 2 loving and supportive parents, the Academy recommends that pediatricians do the following:

• Be familiar with professional literature regarding gay and lesbian parents and their children.

- Support the right of every child and family to the financial, psychologic, and legal security that results from having legally recognized parents who are committed to each other and to the welfare of their children.

- Advocate for initiatives that establish permanency through coparent or second-parent adoption for children of same-sex partners through the judicial system, legislation, and community education.

> *"Mothers and fathers provide crucial things to children that cannot be duplicated in a same-sex household, regardless of the parenting abilities or good intentions of the adults."*

Homosexuals Should Not Have the Right to Adopt

Robert H. Knight

Children should not be placed in foster or adoptive homes headed by homosexuals, argues Robert H. Knight in the following viewpoint. Youths need both a mother and a father to grow up to be stable and healthy adults, he contends. In addition, Knight points out, studies show that children who grow up in homosexual households are more likely to try homosexuality, to be confused about their gender identity, and to be exposed to disease. Knight is director of the Culture and Family Institute of Concerned Women for America, a conservative advocacy organization. This viewpoint is excerpted from testimony Knight delivered before the Virginia Senate on February 16, 2005.

As you read, consider the following questions:

1. According to the National Council on Adoption, cited by Knight, how many married couples are on waiting lists to adopt children?

2. What are the flaws in some of the "gay parenting" studies, according to the author?

Robert H. Knight, testimony before the Courts of Justice Committee, Virginia Senate, February 16, 2005.

3. According to Knight, what do some children of homo-sexual parents have to say about their growing-up experiences?

W e're here to talk about what's best for children and how to secure for them the best possible adoptive homes.

Public policy should be guided not by what some adults want but by what's actually best for children. In most debates, homosexual activists argue that they "deserve" to be parents or that they "want" to be parents. Well, that's understandable. There's a universal longing to be a father or a mother, but this doesn't mean everyone is equally qualified.

The activists also assert that this is about "equality," but that's not true. A household that is missing an entire parental sex, that is, missing a mother or a father, is not equal to a married household.

The Best Chance for a Balanced Life

When placing children in foster homes, the state should do everything in its power to provide the best chance for them to have a balanced, happy home life. A lot of these children come out of a troubled background. They need the best situation. This means finding homes with a married mother and father—not a home with two homosexuals, or a home with two heterosexuals who are unwilling to make a lifelong commitment to each other. Even with the nation's high divorce rate, married homes are far more stable on average than any other model.

This is not about parenting abilities. There are some wonderful single parents who do their best under tough circumstances. But children in single-mother homes can tell you that they don't crave another mom; they want a father. Kids in single-father homes don't crave another daddy; they want a mom.

[Virginia] House Bill No. 2921 wisely seeks to establish public policy that aims to fulfill children's need to have a married mother and a father.

In the popular film *Sleepless in Seattle*, a desperate little boy goes on the radio to seek a wife for his single father. He's already got a great dad, played by Tom Hanks. The boy does not want another dad; he wants a mom. Yet, we're told that public policy should be indifferent to that boy's needs. To put it another way, do we really think the boy would not notice if, instead of getting new mom Meg Ryan, he wound up with a guy from *Queer as Folk* as his "second dad?"

Children Need Mothers and Fathers

It's wrong to place a child in a deliberately motherless or fatherless household, especially when there are married couples waiting to adopt. The National Council on Adoption estimates that between 1 million and 2 million married couples are on waiting lists. They are going to China, Russia and Romania at great expense, seeking children. There is no excuse for placing kids in a motherless or fatherless household or one that isn't even bound by a marital commitment.

Even when a straight, single parent adopts a child, there is at least a chance that a husband or wife will eventually join the parent. But in a homosexual household, there is a deliberate choice to deny a child—for life—of growing up with a father or a mother in the house.

Such a child misses out on viewing, up close, three important relationships: between mothers and fathers, husbands and wives, and men and women, not to mention the special ways in which parents of either sex relate to their sons or daughters.

Who among us could say that our father could be replaced by a lesbian, and this would not have made any difference in our lives? Or that our mother could just as easily have been a male homosexual? Men and women are not interchangeable.

Lower Life Expectancy

We have examined more that 10,000 obituaries of homosexuals: The median age of death for lesbians was in the 40s to 50s; for homosexuals it was in the 40s. Most Americans live into their 70s. Yet in the 1996 U.S. government sex survey the oldest lesbian was 49 years old and the oldest gay 54

Children with homosexual parents are considerably more apt to lose a parent to death. Indeed, a homosexual couple in their 30s is roughly equivalent to a nonhomosexual couple in their late 40s or 50s. Adoption agencies will seldom permit a couple in their late 40s or 50s to adopt a child because of the risk of parental death, and the consequent social and psychological difficulty for the child. The AAP [American Academy of Pediatrics] did not address this fact—one with profound implications for any child legally related to a homosexual.

Paul Cameron, Insight on the News, *April 22, 2002.*

Mothers and fathers provide crucial things to children that cannot be duplicated in a same-sex household, regardless of the parenting abilities or good intentions of the adults. Every child deserves a first-class adoption, not to become the object of a politically-driven social experiment.

"Gay Parenting" Studies Are Flawed

Homosexual activists and their allies at professional organizations often assert that "science" has proved that children are no different if raised in homosexual households. The American Academy of Pediatrics (AAP) even released a statement to this effect, and featured an article in an AAP journal by a pro-homosexual researcher as the foundation for its assessment.

This researcher showed her biases right up front by describing marriage itself as a "heterosexist" institution. So much for objective science.

Most "gay parenting" studies compare children in lesbian households with children in heterosexual, single-mother households. The only major study to directly compare children raised in married, single-parent and same-sex households was published by the journal *Children Australia*, and it revealed that, "Overall, the study has shown that children of married couples are more likely to do well at school, in academic and social terms, than children of cohabiting heterosexual and homosexual couples."

The "gay parenting" studies, as a whole, are extremely flawed, with all but a handful written by pro-homosexual researchers. In *No Basis: What the studies Don't tell us about same-sex parenting*, authors Robert Lerner and Althea Nagai demonstrate that all of these studies are "gravely deficient," with some having self-selected sample sizes of less than a dozen people. Earlier, the *Journal of Divorce & Remarriage* examined a number of "gay parenting" studies and reported: "The conclusion that there are no significant differences in children reared by lesbian mothers versus heterosexual mothers is not supported by the published research data base."

One of the most frequently cited researchers, Charlotte Patterson of the University of Virginia, a lesbian who often testifies in adoption and custody cases, was rebuked by a Florida court for failing to reveal how she documented her findings. The court, by the way, upheld Florida's law barring homosexuals from adopting, and that verdict was recently upheld by the U.S. Supreme Court.

Youths in Same-Sex Households

In 2001, a team of pro-homosexual researchers from the University of Southern California did a meta-analysis of "gay parenting" studies and published a refreshingly honest article in *American Sociological Review*. "(How) Does the Sexual Orientation of Parents Matter?" The authors concluded that, yes, studies show that girls are more likely to "be sexually adventurous and less chaste," including being more likely to try lesbianism, and that boys are more likely to have "fluid" conceptions of gender roles, and that researchers should stop trying to cover this up in the hopes of pursuing a pro-homosexual agenda. The researchers said, in effect: *Some of the kids are more likely to turn out gay or bisexual, but so what?*

Even with all their statistical shortcomings, the parenting studies, as a whole, show that children raised in same-sex households are more likely to view homosexuality positively, try homosexuality themselves, or to suffer gender identity confusion. This makes sense; children's most important role models are their parents. If homosexual behavior is offered to them as normal on a daily basis, more of them are going to think it is normal and desirable.

In an often-quoted study by Susan Golombok and Fiona Tasker, the authors note that the "large majority of children who grew up in lesbian households identified as heterosexual." But another of their findings is often ignored: "Those who had grown up in a lesbian family were more likely to consider the possibility of having lesbian or gay relationships, and to actually do so." The authors conclude that growing up in a lesbian household's "accepting atmosphere" of homosexuality "may facilitate the development of a lesbian or gay sexual orientation for some individuals. But, interestingly, the opportunity to explore same-sex relationships may, for others, confirm their heterosexual identity."

Health Risks of Homosexuality

Since there is no credible scientific evidence that homosexuality is genetic, it makes sense that kids exposed to parental homosexuality will tend to see it as a viable option. This is tragic, since homosexuality has well-documented health risks, especially for young men, but also for young women.

Various medical journals report drastically higher incidences of sexually transmitted diseases, shortened life spans, domestic violence, alcohol and drug abuse, and psychological problems among homosexuals. San Francisco and New York health authorities are now grappling with a new strain of HIV that is resistant to drug treatments and can result in full-blown AIDS within a year or two instead of the usual 10-year incubation. They're also greatly alarmed by a new strain of Chlamydia among young homosexual men that is resisting treatment.

Homosexuality aside, it should be no mystery that children need and want both a mother and a father; it's a self-evident truth. It follows that public policy ought to encourage placement of children in married households.

Some children of homosexual parents are beginning to speak out and contradict the idea that it's the same as being raised with a mom and dad. I have heard from several people raised by homosexuals who have told me that they are still dealing, years later, with family dysfunction. One woman poignantly related how she felt when she came out of her bedroom one night and saw her father kiss his male lover on the lips. She said she was physically ill and to this day needs counseling.

Emily's Story

Here's a letter we received at Concerned Women for America from a woman named Emily:

> Thank you, thank you, thank you for all that you are doing to protect children from being placed in homosexual households. I spent part of my teenage years living with my mother and her female lover. It was a heartbreaking and disturbing experience to say the least. The needs of the children MUST be placed before the desires of adults. Through-

out my life, the most well-balanced and successful people I encounter come from healthy, loving, traditional families. I wish I did too!

In conclusion, let me pose a scenario that, I hope, will put this into perspective. Most of you here are married and have children. If something happened to you and your spouse, would you be comfortable having your son placed in a house with two homosexual men, or a house with two lesbians? How about your daughter being placed with two lesbians, or with two homosexual men?

If those scenarios trouble you as to your own children, why would it be okay for other people's children? The state of Virginia owes all foster children a first-class adoption, nothing less.

"Embryonic adoption should be preferred in the law always over destroying human embryos for stem-cell research."

Embryo Adoption Should Be Encouraged

Jonathan Imbody

The extra embryos created by in vitro fertilization (IVF) procedures should be adopted to prevent their destruction by researchers, argues Jonathan Imbody in the following viewpoint. These embryos are fully human, and it is immoral to sacrifice them for even well-intentioned stem cell experiments, Imbody asserts. Moreover, while embryonic research has not yet produced any medical cures, embryonic adoption offers the gift of life to unborn children and infertile couples, he maintains. Imbody is a senior policy analyst for the Christian Medical Association.

As you read, consider the following questions:

1. According to Suzanne Murray, what dehumanizing language has been used to describe human embryos?
2. What percentage of IVF embryos have been frozen, according to the author?
3. According to Gene Rudd, how can the problem of "excess" embryos be resolved?

Jonathan Imbody, "Embryo Adoption: A Win-Win," *National Right to Life News,* vol. 31, October 2004, p. 18. Copyright © 2004 National Right to Life Committee, Inc. Reproduced by permission.

At a time when Congress is fiercely debating whether to protect human embryos or destroy them for research, a handful of squirming, laughing, crying, and sleeping toddlers offered convincing evidence for their right to life.

The families who spoke at the U.S. Capitol on September 22 [2004] are part of a growing movement that provides a humane alternative to disposing of or conducting research on "excess" human embryos created by in vitro fertilization (IVF). It's called "embryo adoption."

One of the sponsors of the gathering, Sen. Rick Santorum (R-Pa.), said the purpose of the program "is to take these little children and give them the potential to live the rest of their lives as the gifts from God that they are."

Fully Human

Congressman Mike Pence (R-In.) praised the gathering. "Now why would people come from Berne, Indiana?" he asked. "Well, the answer can be found in their 18-month-old twins Caroline and Spencer who are a daily and profound reminder that embryonic adoption should be preferred in the law always over destroying human embryos for stem-cell research."

Cong. Pence added, "You see, Caroline and Spencer Keim are fully human today, just as they were 18 short months ago when they were in the frozen embryonic stage of their development. They stand as a living testament to the truth that it would have been morally wrong to destroy their embryonic lives even for well-intentioned medical research."

One mother after another took turns at a press conference sponsored by Focus on the Family to explain why legislators should view their children, each adopted in the embryo stage, as human beings—not as fodder for lethal experiments. Families also voiced strong opposition to The Stem Cell Research Enhancement Act of 2004 (H.R. 4682) a bill to require federal funding of stem cell research that requires killing IVF-created human embryos.

"Human Embryos Are Not 'Goldfish'"

Suzanne Murray, a nurse who along with husband, Peter, adopted their daughter Mary as an embryo, recalled a September 14, 2000, hearing of the Senate Appropriations Committee on embryonic stem cell research.

Mrs. Murray noted, "Senator Tom Harkin of Iowa and actress Mary Tyler Moore used dehumanizing and demeaning language to describe our daughter, Mary." She continued, "You see, on that day, Mary was an embryo whose future was in frozen suspension. Without knowing her or considering her humanity during this vulnerable stage of development, Sen. Harkin referred to our Mary as a 'dot.' Ms. Moore likened our daughter to a 'goldfish.'"

But human embryos are not "dots" or "goldfish," Mrs. Murray said, "and Mary stands before you today as proof."

A Cure for Everyone Involved

While some researchers lobbying Congress to fund destructive embryonic stem cell research have dangled cures in front of desperate patients, not everyone is rising to the bait.

As adoptive mother of a two-year-old, Kate Johnson explained that she and her husband, Steve, were unable to conceive because of a spinal injury Steve suffered in a bicycle accident. "Some proponents of destructive embryonic stem cell research, like [actor] Christopher Reeve,[1] point to their disabilities as a reason to destroy frozen embryos for stem cells," she said. "For Steve, all he has to do is look at our daughter Zara, who would not be here with us today if someone had dissected her for embryonic stem cell research."

Mrs. Johnson added, "In reality, it is more likely that Steve's paralysis will be reversed using adult stem cells, as evidenced by a recent Senate hearing featuring two paralyzed women who can now walk with the aid of walkers thanks to adult stem cell therapies."

1. Reeve died on October 11, 2004.

Embryo Adoption Versus Traditional Adoption

The most obvious difference between an embryo adoption and a traditional adoption is the pregnancy experience. Adoptive moms are able to experience the joys (and burdens!) of pregnancy and labor. You have the peace of mind of knowing your child was not exposed to alcohol or drugs during pregnancy.

Although an embryo adoption allows more control in some ways, it provides less in other ways. You cannot choose the gender of the child as you might in an international or older child adoption, and you can't change your mind and not accept the baby if he or she is born with a medical or developmental illness or condition. In addition, because up to three embryos are implanted at once, you might have twins or triplets. Embryo adoption can also be more difficult emotionally than traditional adoption, since there is no guarantee that in the end you will have a child.

Nightlight Christian Adoptions,
"Snowflakes Frozen Embryo Adoption,"
Frequently Asked Questions, www.nightlight.org.

Adoptive mother Sharon Tesdall agreed. "Embryonic stem cell research has not successfully treated a single patient, and there is no promise of it ever doing so," she said. "While some want to destroy IVF embryos in the pursuit of treating some medical conditions, we advocate using IVF embryos to treat another medical condition: infertility."

Mrs. Tesdall argued that embryo adoption "provides a 'cure' for everyone involved," most importantly, "the child whose gift of life is realized."

Lifesaving Alternatives

Ronald Stoddart, executive director of Nightlight Christian Adoptions—the organization that facilitated the embryo adoption of the children present at the press conference—lamented the ethical and economic dark side of in vitro fertilization.

"Couples who create embryos through IVF do so at an expense of tens of thousands of dollars and an emotional roller coaster ride," Stoddart observed. "Although the genetic parents plan to use 88 percent of these embryos for future attempts to build their family, 12 percent are literally in frozen orphanages. Some refer to this 12 percent as 'excess embryos.' The word, 'excess,' is dehumanizing and inaccurate."

A study of 217 in vitro fertilization clinics across the country, reported [in October 2004] by the University of Pennsylvania and Rutgers University, noted that fertility clinics vary widely in what they do with frozen human embryos from IVF procedures who are not implanted into a mother.

University of Penn bioethicist Arthur Caplan, who was part of the team that conducted the survey, told the Associated Press, "I don't think anyone who deals with these frozen embryos considers them to be persons. But I think that they feel they are deserving of respect. . . . They see the potential for life in this material."

Gene Rudd, M.D., an obstetrician and associate executive director of the Christian Medical Association (CMA), scoffed at such hedging.

"Saying that they 'respect' them while then proceeding to kill them for the sake of other ambitions is illogical and dispassionate," Dr. Rudd asserted. He said that to resolve the problem of so-called "excess" embryos, CMA has "called for parents undergoing reproductive technologies to allow the in vitro process to produce only the number of embryos they are committed to implant now or later, regardless of whether successful pregnancy is achieved early in the process. Our embryos are no less our responsibility than our born children."

A Win-Win Situation

Dr. Rudd explained that CMA has fostered the establishment of the National Embryo Donation Center to link embryos with adopting parents and to provide the reproductive technologies necessary for them to have the chance to be born.

As adoptive mother Cara Vest noted, "IVF parents have a moral responsibility to their offspring that cannot be fulfilled by donating them for research or discarding them as medical waste." Embryo adoption, she concluded, "is a win-win for everyone involved."

| *"This kind of adoption actually destroys far more embryos than it saves."*

Supporting Embryo Adoption Is Hypocritical

Michael Ennis

Religious conservatives often claim that embryonic stem cell research is immoral because it destroys the embryo, a vulnerable and precious form of human life. Some conservatives contend that the excess embryos created for in vitro fertilization (IVF) procedures should be adopted and given life rather than be destroyed by stem cell research. In the following viewpoint Michael Ennis explains that these adoptions also involve IVF procedures, which always result in the destruction of numerous embryos. Thus, he concludes, it is hypocritical to suggest that embryo adoption is a moral choice but that embryonic stem cell research is not. Ennis is a writer for Texas Monthly *magazine.*

As you read, consider the following questions:

1. What percentage of the U.S. population is opposed to in vitro fertilization, according to Ennis?

2. According to the author, what is the Snowflakes program?

3. About how many frozen embryos would have to be destroyed in order for three thousand embryos to be adopted, according to Ennis?

When Congress threatened to loosen limits on stem cell research earlier [in 2005], the Bush administration called in the snowflakes. Rescued as embryos from fertility clinic freezers by families who had "adopted" them and brought them to parturition (legally speaking, children have to be born before they can be adopted), these previously frozen test-tube babies were invited to the White House [in May 2005] for some well-publicized cuddling with the president. Wearing "Former Embryo" T-shirts, the adorable thawed tots allowed the administration to make a point about the hundreds of thousands of spare embryos currently chilling in liquid nitrogen at clinics around the nation, many of them destined to be thrown out or, if new legislation is passed, destroyed in taxpayer-financed research. "Rather than discard these embryos created during in vitro fertilization," observed President Bush, "or turn them over for research that destroys them, these families have chosen a life-affirming alternative."

Fuzzy Ethics

The fate of frozen embryos has become one of our most pressing public issues, central not only to the debate over stem cell research but also to a wider culture war between science and faith. To religious conservatives intent on building a "culture of life," these microscopic bundles of eight or so undifferentiated cells are cryogenically suspended human lives crying out for our protection. To many other Americans across a wide ideological spectrum—from liberal bioethicists to conservative Republicans like Senate majority leader Dr. Bill Frist—the frozen embryos are full genetic blueprints for human beings sadly destined never to develop but capable of saving countless lives. Religious conservatives have scrambled to throw embryo adoption into the fray because it seems to provide living proof that each one of these frozen souls, certain to perish if its stem cells are extracted for research, is already on the way to becoming a camera-ready kid. In the cold light of day, however, the picture isn't so heartwarming: This kind of adoption actually destroys far more embryos than it saves. Behind the holier-than-thou claims for this alternative, which already receives taxpayer support, there's nothing but fuzzy ethics, a moral calculus that just doesn't add up.

In Vitro Fertilization

To do the math properly, you have to start with this date: July 25, 1978. That's the birthday of an English girl who overcame long odds to become the first so-called test-tube baby (she was actually conceived in a petri dish). Louise Brown was the 200th in a sacrificial lineage of fertilized eggs that researchers attempted to implant in a woman's uterus before she was brought to term. But researchers quickly learned how to make in vitro fertilization (IVF) more efficient and affordable. Fertility-enhancing drugs could stimulate the ovaries to over-produce eggs, and several fertilized eggs could be implanted in the womb at one time, increasing the chance that at least one would result in a live birth. Because delicately removing the unfertilized eggs from the ovaries is the most expensive part of the process, it became more economical to remove a large number—ideally about fifteen—during each extraction procedure and to implant two to four in the womb after they had been fertilized. The spares could then be cryogenically frozen for future implantations. The first birth from a thawed embryo was in 1984; today, thousands of babies are born from frozen embryos every year.

Also born on Louise's birthday was one of modern medicine's most unlikely success stories. Although IVF is expensive (averaging about $12,000 for each egg extraction "cycle"), not particularly reliable (even with multiple embryo implantations, the chance of a live birth is about one in three), and usually not covered by insurance in this country, it has become a multibillion-dollar industry, accounting for one in every hundred American births; Today, IVF seems to be one of the few things most Americans agree on. A recent Harris poll showed that only 10 percent of the population had a religious prohibition against IVF, a figure that was similar to the one for those who objected to routine surgery.

Mixed Messages

But religious leaders have never given petri-dish procreation such an overwhelming mandate. Lacking direct scriptural guidance, they've adopted a make-it-up-as-you-go approach to the morality of IVF, and their messages have often been mixed. Despite some early misgivings, assisted reproduction was rather quickly accepted by many influential Christian conservatives; the Christian Medical and Dental Associations endorsed IVF within the bounds of marriage in 1983. Focus on the Family founder James Dobson, who recently compared embryonic stem cell research to Nazi medical experiments, summarized evangelical Protestant pragmatism on IVF: "I feel that in vitro fertilization is less problematic when the donors are husband and wife—if all the fertilized eggs are inserted into the uterus. . . . As the woman's body then accepts one or more eggs and rejects the others, the process is left in God's hands. This seems to violate no moral principles."

However, IVF did violate the moral principles of the Roman Catholic Church. In 1987 the Congregation for the Doctrine of Faith (a more benign successor to the dreaded inquisition) issued a landmark document known as "Donum Vitae" ("The Gift of Life"), which proscribed IVF because of the embryo attrition and because even married couples' using their own eggs offended "the dignity of procreation and of the conjugal union." The author of "Donum Vitae" was Cardinal Joseph Ratzinger—now Pope Benedict XVI—and his thinking was instrumental in shaping his predecessor's epochal 1995 encyclical "The Gospel of Life." Directly quoting Ratzinger's "Donum Vitae," Pope John Paul II insisted that "the human being is to be respected and treated as a person from the mo-

Do Embryos Need Protection?

For the federal government to fund programs to exclusively encourage [embryo] donation to other couples is to use public money to endorse a particular view about the status of embryos and what should be done with them.

Most important, it is a step away from couples controlling the fate of their embryos, and toward viewing embryos as needing government protection and the help of groups that seek to "place" them with caring families. The way we're heading, it's a short step to lab freezers being called orphanages, and social workers assigned to look after the interests of their frozen charges. Is it cold in here, or is it just me?

Jeffrey P. Kahn, "'Adoption' of Frozen Embryos a Loaded Term," September 17, 2002, www.cnn.com.

ment of conception." Noting that even free societies have approved of euthanasia, abortion, and capital punishment, the pontiff declared, "We are facing an enormous and dramatic clash between good and evil, death and life, the 'culture of death' and the 'culture of life.'"

The late pope's catchphrase first appeared in our political arena when George W. Bush started talking about the culture of life in his 2000 campaign. Not only has our born-again Methodist president popularized the pithy pontifical slogan, but he also precisely echoes the language and theology of "The Gospel of Life" while continuing to disagree with the Vatican on capital punishment, preemptive war, and, as it turns out, IVF, for which the president has taken pains to reiterate his support.

As the culture of life bounced along unpredictably from the mind of the future pope to the pen of the late pope to the mouth of our president, the freezers were filling with frozen embryos. An oft-cited RAND Corporation study from 2002 identified almost 400,000 "frosties," as they're known in the trade, of which almost 90 percent were being kept in cold storage for future implantations by their biological parents. Of the rest, about 11,000 had been donated for biomedical research, which could yield an estimated 275 new "lines" for embryonic stem cell research (the Bush administration currently approves 22 preexisting lines for federally funded research). About 9,000 embryos have been designated as available for "donation" (the term the fertility industry prefers) to other couples, with an equal number expected to be discarded.

The Snowflakes Program

The concept of adopting some of these frozen embryos originated with California-based Nightlight Christian Adoptions, which started its Snowflakes program in 1997. (Frosties were dubbed "snowflakes" to emphasize that each embryo is a genetically unique human.) Even before President Bush made his 2001 decision allowing research only on embryonic stem cell lines that had already been extracted from discarded embryos—thus avoiding the "further destruction of human embryos that have at least the potential for life"—some of Snowflakes' clients had trundled their babies to congressional offices and lobbied against embryonic stem cell research. Since 2002, the U.S. Department of Health and Human Services has distributed millions of dollars in federal grants to promote "public awareness" of the adoption option, with most of the money going to Snowflakes and another Christian-affiliated program.

That awareness was greatly increased when 21 Snowflakes families, both adopters and donors, met the president at the May [2005] photo op. According to Snowflakes' own figures, at about that time 120 client families had thawed 985 contractually adopted embryos, of which a bit more than half weren't viable after being defrosted—the average rate of attrition for the IVF industry. About half of the client families eventually ended up with a total of 81 children (twins and triplets, the result of those multiple implantations, are common in IVF), again an average success rate. But that's roughly a ten-to-one ratio of dead embryos to living children, a rather costly "rescue," to use a term ubiquitous in adoption circles, of embryos that weren't in any imminent danger in the deep freeze; their donors, who must give consent to any transfer of their embryos, could instead have opted to keep them frozen. (A California baby was recently born after thirteen years at minus 319 degrees.)

Shortly before meeting with the lucky snowflakes who survived their rescues, the president told reporters he would exercise the first veto of his tenure if Congress passed a bill to lift restrictions on embryonic stem cell research. He rejected using "taxpayers' money to promote science which destroys life in order to save life" but just three days later, the president was lauding a program that uses taxpayers' money to promote the destruction of a lot of embryos in order to save a few. And it would be mass destruction if somehow all the 29,000 embryos destined for research, donation, or discarding were put up for adoption (in practice the vast majority of couples don't like the idea of someone else raising their genetic offspring). Currently, the cost of rescuing perhaps 3,000 snowflakes would be more than 25,000 "innocent human lives."

Cynical Duplicity

But the White House is hardly alone in advancing the fuzzy ethical concept that an embryo is absolutely, positively an inviolable human life—except when it needs to be sacrificed to make the point that it is absolutely, positively an inviolable human life. Powerful conservative Christian organizations such as the Family Research Council, which had pilloried the president for his indifference to human life after his 2001 decision, have leaped to embrace embryo adoption. Remarkably, even the Catholic Church waffles on this one; almost two decades after ruling that IVF performed with donor embryos (the essential procedure in embryo adoption) is even more illicit than using your own, the Vatican continues to insist that it needs more "scientific and statistical data" before making a ruling on embryo adoption. Little wonder that some skeptics believe that embryo adoption is a back door to criminalizing abortion: If a day-old embryo could be legally adopted as a living person under the law—currently only property law applies—then every fetus would acquire the legal status of a person.

However, for the culture of life to be absolutely, positively consistent on the inviolability of the embryo, religious conservatives across the board would have to suck it up and attack IVF as aggressively as they have abortion rights. That would result in the spectacle of embryo rights protesters descending on Washington, waving blurry gray microscope photos of amorphous eight-cell clusters, while thousands of adorable kids and accomplished young adults counterprotest in T-shirts reading "Former Test-Tube Baby." Given IVF's already overwhelming public support, who do you think is going to win that confrontation—and why are we not likely to see it?

So our frozen embryos remain in liquid nitrogen limbo, their status morally ambiguous even to religious conservatives who so starkly contrast their culture of life with the confused moral "relativism" of a secular culture of death. Of course, the object of embryo adoption is humane and high-minded, but it is no more or less so—and no more or lass deadly to embryos—than the compassionate goals of embryonic stem cell research; it's the hypocrisy with which the distinction has been made that should raise more than a minor alarm. At a time when we are increasingly outsourcing our public and private morality to a consortium of powerful institutions—the megachurches, televangelical ministries, advocacy groups like

Focus on the Family, and the White House—we are in danger of building a culture of life crafted, at best, with careless naivete and, at worst, with glib political slogans and cynical duplicity.

Periodical Bibliography

The following articles have been selected to supplement the diverse views presented in this chapter.

Samiya A. Bashir	"The Best Interest of the Child," *ColorLines*, Winter 2002/2003.
Peter Beresford	"Wisdom of Solomon," *Community Care*, June 9, 2005.
Sherry Boschert	"Challenge Posed by Foreign Adoptees," *Pediatric News*, May 2002.
Brian Connelly	"The Problem Behind Chinese Adoptions," *American Enterprise*, January/February 2004.
Candi Cushman	"He Has No Mama Now," *Citizen*, January 2003.
Amy Dickinson	"Bicultural Kids: Parents Who Adopt Children of a Different Ethnicity Are Enjoying the Best of Both Worlds," *Time*, August 26, 2002.
E.J. Graff	"The Other Marriage War: There's One Group That Is Pursuing Legal Union—and Its Kids Need the Stability," *American Prospect*, April 8, 2002.
Albert R. Hunt	"Blocking Gay Adoption Hurts Kids," *Wall Street Journal*, March 21, 2002.
Claude Knobler	"Understanding Love: When We Adopted Nati from Ethiopia, We Discovered That Language Isn't Always Necessary to Connect," *Parenting*, September 1, 2005.
Rod Liddle	"Only Blacks Need Apply," *Spectator*, November 2, 2002.
Celeste McGovern	"Tangled Web of Embryo Adoption," *Report*, March 31, 2003.
Dorothy Roberts	"Racial Harm," *ColorLines*, Fall 2002.

OPPOSING VIEWPOINTS® SERIES

CHAPTER 4

Which Adoption Policies Should Be Supported?

Chapter Preface

B efore the late 1960s most infant adoptions in the United States were "closed," or confidential. Closed adoptions generally ensured that the identity of the biological parents was retained in sealed records and kept secret from the adoptee and the adoptive family. Likewise, biological parents could not retrieve information on the child they had surrendered for adoption.

In the earlier part of the twentieth century, confidential adoption was perceived as the best solution to an out-of-wedlock pregnancy. Instead of having an abortion or raising a child who, in that era, would be stigmatized as illegitimate, the biological mother could relinquish the child and be reassured that he or she would grow up in a "legitimate" two-parent family. The birth mother would also be released from the stigma of unwed motherhood and be given the chance for later marriage and respectable parenthood. In addition, adoptive parents faced with infertility would be able to have children denied to them by biology, and adoptees would be afforded the stability and opportunities that family provides. Keeping the identity of the biological parents secret was seen as a way to protect the parents from pain and scandal. Many also believed that it ensured the permanence of the adoptive family.

In recent years, a growing number of adoptees and birth parents have advocated for the opening of sealed adoption records. As this volume goes to press, six states allow adoptees unrestricted access to their records; in most other states adult adoptees must obtain court permission to view their original birth certificates. Advocates for open records maintain that adoptees have the right to know the circumstances of their birth and the identity of their biological parents. Beyond the possible need for medical information, many adoptees feel haunted by questions about their background, supporters note. "I think it is unreasonable to ask any human being to divorce themselves from the facts of their own birth," says Denise K. Castelluci, founder of Voices of Adoption. "Interest or disinterest in one's own origins should be a personal decision of the individual, not a decision made by government or any other individual," she asserts.

Although open-records advocates enjoy a high level of public support, some adoption experts express reservations about making formerly private records readily available. The biological mother may need to keep her information confidential, they note. As syndicated columnist Marianne Means points out, mothers generally relinquish their children "for sad and humiliating but compelling reasons. The babies may be illegitimate, the result of horrific rape, or simply a financial and emotional burden that a poor family or teen-age mother cannot assume." Means fears that if the confidentiality of a birth mother's identity cannot be ensured, women with unwanted pregnancies may choose abortion over adoption. "The open-records movement is so young we don't have proof yet that it encourages abortion. But common sense says it will," Means concludes.

The controversy over adoptees' access to their birth records will likely continue as a growing number of states take up the issue in their legislatures or at the ballot box. The authors in the following chapter examine how new laws and policies may affect adoption and whether or not such changes are necessary.

| "*An adopted child whose birthfamily and adoptive family come together in a familial way will grow up with greater certainty.*"

Open Adoption Policies Should Be Supported

Brenda Romanchik

Brenda Romanchik is the author of several books about birth parents and adoption, including Birthparent Grief *and* Finding Our Place: Birthparents in Open Adoptions. *In the following viewpoint Romanchik contends that maintaining ongoing relationships between birth parents, adoptees, and adoptive parents can be the most beneficial arrangement for all involved. Open adoption creates a blended family that undoubtedly will face challenges but that can also provide love, stability, and a sense of wholeness for the adopted child, she maintains.*

As you read, consider the following questions:

1. What does Romanchik mean by "philosophy of comfort"? Why is it counterproductive in the adoption process, in her opinion?

2. What are the two main advantages of open adoption, according to the author?

3. According to Romanchik, what other kind of familial relationship is open adoption comparable to?

Ask five people what their definition of open adoption is and you are likely to get five answers. Some may think that allowing an expectant parent to choose the prospective adoptive parents from a profile of non-identifying information is an open adoption. Still others may say that those who met prior to placement and who exchange pictures and letters after the child is placed in the adoptive home are participating in an open adoption. This definition is, in fact, a variation of a *semiopen adoption* or *openness in adoption*.

So what is an open adoption? The primary difference between a truly open adoption and a semi-open adoption is that *the adopted child has the potential of developing a one-on-one relationship with his or her birthfamily*. It is not about the adoptive parents bestowing birthparents with the privilege of contact, nor is it about birthparents merely being available to provide information over the years. Direct contact, in the form of letters, phone calls and visits between the *birthfamily* and the adopted child, along with his adoptive family, is essential if they are to establish their own relationship. After all, how can we honestly call an adoption open if the child is not involved?

For many who are just beginning the adoption process, the concept of open adoption appears to be another complication they would rather not deal with. One prospective adoptive mom, weary from years of infertility, asked me at an adoption conference, "I am pursuing an international adoption because I don't want to have to deal with my child's birthfamily in any way. What can you say to me that would make me change my mind and pursue, instead, an open adoption?" My answer to her was simply this: "No matter where your child is adopted from, you will, as adoptive parents, need to 'deal with' your child's birthfamily whether you know the birthfamily or not. This birthfamily is a part of who your child is. Open adoption allows you to know your child better by knowing his birthfamily."

Expectant parents considering placing a child for adoption are often just as leery of the prospect of open adoption. Many are told, or feel, that ongoing contact will make it difficult to move on with their lives. Some are afraid that seeing their child will be too painful. Many worry that their involvement might confuse the child

Making Open Adoption Child-Centered

Many adoptive professionals encourage prospective birthparents and adoptive parents in the pre-placement process to choose the level of contact "they are most comfortable with having." The philosophy of comfort does not take into consideration several very important factors, one being that open adoption should not be based on making the adults involved comfortable; rather it should be about providing for the needs of the child. Much of the open adoption experience is uncomfortable and awkward, especially in the beginning. While it is true that many children are only as comfortable as the adults around them, it is also true that many of us do things for our children that we are not totally comfortable with because it is good for them.

The other factor that the philosophy of comfort does not take into consideration is that adoption is a lifelong process. Many birthparents in the crisis of planning for an adoption look upon continuing contact as an option too painful to contemplate. Many adoptive parents, on the other hand, just want to be a family, without the added complication of visits with their child's birthfamily. Most open adoption agreements are based on these feelings that occur around the time of placement. These agreements do not allow contact to ebb and flow according to the needs of all involved, most importantly the child. As time goes on, many birthparents, adoptive parents, and the adopted child find they want more contact, but feel they are not able to ask for more because of the original agreement. In cases such as these open adoption becomes a contract instead of a covenant.

According to Webster's Revised Unabridged Dictionary, covenant is defined in part as being one of the strongest and most solemn forms of contract. It is also described as being sacred. For open adoption to work best, birthparents and adoptive parents need to see their involvement with each other as a sacred commitment, or a covenant they make to each other for the sake of the child.

A Form of Blended Family

Patricia Martinez Domer, author of *Children of Open Adoption* and *Talking to Your Child About Adoption*, encourages us to see open adoption as just another form of blended family. In adopting, adoptive parents are welcoming the member of one family into their own. This "blending" of families is not without its share of uncomfortable moments, but the beauty of birthparents and adoptive parents accepting each other as family is twofold:

One, birthparents and adoptive parents really get to know each other. It allows them to see who the others are outside of their adoption experience. Birthparents can be seen as more than someone who found themselves in a difficult situation and adoptive parents can be seen as more than an infertile couple. Being able to know each other as complete human beings allows for greater acceptance. The adopted child is also able to know his birthparents as they are, rather than creating a fantasy birthparent. Instead of spending countless hours conjuring up an image of a person they do not know, they can use that energy for other things.

Two, it gives the child a sense of wholeness. There will no doubt be times when birthparents and adoptive parents take up the responsibility of maintaining the connection with each other. An infant, a toddler or a child cannot carry the burden

Closed vs. Open Adoptions: Benefits for Adoptees

	Confidential Adoptions	Semi-Open Adoptions	Open Adoptions
Description	No contact between birth and adoptive families. No identifying information is provided.	Non-identifying contact, via letters and pictures, through an agency or attorney.	Direct interaction between birth and adoptive families. Identities are known.
Benefits for Adoptees	Protection from unstable, abusive, or emotionally disturbed birth parents.	Genetic and birth history are known. Birth parents are "real" and not "fantasy." Positive adjustment is promoted in adoptee.	Direct access to birth parents and history. Identity questions are answered. (Who do I look like? Why was I placed?) Eases feelings of abandonment. Increased circle of supportive adults. Exposure to racial and ethnic heritage. Lessens loyalty conflicts.

SOURCE: National Adoption Information Clearinghouse, June 17, 2004. http://naic.acf.hhs.gov.

of maintaining the connection between his two families. An adopted child whose birthfamily and adoptive family come together in a familial way will grow up with greater certainty. There is a saying that the greatest gift parents can give their children is to love one another. I think it is inclusive of all parents, not just married couples.

Relationship Vary

So, what does a family blended by open adoption best compare to? In their book, *The Open Adoption Experience*, Sharon Kaplan-Roszia and Lois Melina state: "In practice, the relationship in open adoption is . . . comparable to that between in-laws."

In marriage, a spouse accepts his or her in-laws because he or she realizes that they are an important part of who his or her spouse is. In open adoption, the adoptive family and birthfamily make a commitment to stay in contact because they also realize that the birthfamily is an important part of who the child is. As with in-laws, relationships vary. Some open adoption relationships develop into friendships while others are more distantly involved. All, however, recognize that they are family to one another, and important in the life of the child.

| "Adoptive parents are not ethically bound to include birth parents in their lives."

Open Adoptions Are Not for Everyone

Anita L. Allen

Open adoptions, in which birth families and adoptive families are known to each other and maintain contact, are generally a positive development, writes Anita L. Allen in the following viewpoint. Yet open adoptions are not feasible in all cases, she points out. Adoptive parents may find it too inconvenient or painful to include birth parents in their extended families, she explains. The adoptive parents are ultimately the legal caretakers of the adoptee and should not be condemned if they prefer to forego contact with the biological parents, Allen concludes. Allen is a professor of law and philosophy at the University of Pennsylvania.

As you read, consider the following questions:

1. What are "time-limited" and "mediated" open adoptions, according to Allen?

2. In the author's view, what was confusing and stressful about Sue and Brad's relationship with the birth parents of their adopted child?

3. What are adopted parents obligated to do, in Allen's opinion?

Adoption is undergoing significant change. "Open" adoption—also called "disclosed" and "cooperative" adoption—is gaining acceptance. The adoptions between strangers that took place in the United States in the decades after World War II were unduly "closed." The parties were anonymous, the procedures were confidential, the official records were sealed. In addition, birth parents legally transferred all parental rights and responsibilities respecting their offspring and were then expected to drop out of sight. Most did. The experts of yesteryear maintained that closed adoption hastened the end of birth mothers' grief, spared them shame, enabled them to go on with their lives, and ensured that their offspring would grow up with secure identities. Experts also maintained that closed adoptions would allow adoptive parents to maintain secrecy and bond more early with their adopted children.

The closed adoption regime and its ideologies of secrecy and shame are fading. A growing number of adoption professionals and legal experts now believe that the birth parents of children placed for adoption should not be forced out of sight and should be permitted to maintain a relationship with their offspring. Although some birth parents prefer that the legal termination of parental rights and responsibilities also terminate their relationship with their offspring and the adopting families, other birth parents welcome post-adoption contacts. Many adoptive parents reportedly value the information about their children's health and origins that contact with birth parents affords. Research by Harold D. Grotevant and Ruth G. McRoy discredits assumptions of the old, closed adoption regime. Dozens of adoptive parents, birth parents, and adoptees interviewed over a period of years report good experiences with open adoptions, including what Grotevant and McRoy refer to as "time-limited" and agency "mediated" open adoptions. "Time-limited" open adoptions are those in which the parties agree that for a limited time before and after birth, birth parents will have contact with the adoptive family. "Mediated" open adoptions are those in which the ongoing contact that birth parents have with the adoptive family is arranged or supervised by an adoption agency. . . .

Concerns About Open Adoptions

Although greater openness in adoption has been a positive development, openness generates a number of difficult practical, ethical, and legal concerns. Legal concerns include whether courts must enforce open adoption agreements and whether authorities should unseal adoption records. Practical concerns include whether adoption agencies can effectively mediate potential conflicts between communicating birth and adoptive families. Ethical concerns include the limits of birth parents' responsibilities to provide information about their health, genes, and families to adoptive families. One ethical concern goes straight to the heart of the very idea of post-placement open adoption arrangements in domestic adoptions: whether adoptive parents are ethically bound significantly to include birth parents in their lives, after an otherwise successful placement and termination of birth parents' legal rights.

Excluding the Birth Parents: An Illustration

Should birth parents ever be excluded? Sue and Brad are the parents of two children, Sam and Lynn, whom they adopted as infants several years apart. Sam's adoption, their first, was facilitated by an agency that placed children anonymously and confidentially. Sue and Brad did not meet Sam's birth parents. Lynn's adoption, their second, was facilitated by an agency that encouraged open adoption practices. The agency asked birth parents to participate in the selection of adoptive parents. The agency encouraged prospective adoptive parents to meet birth parents and offer to provide letters and photographs throughout the child's life.

The Problem with Open Adoptions

There is mounting evidence that open adoption has not addressed the needs of the people who place, and there are increasing complaints that adoptive parents are not fulfilling agreements for contact they made prior to the adoption finalization, indicating that open adoption arrangements have not been satisfactory for adoptive families. There are efforts in some states to pass legislation requiring adoptive parents to comply with prefinalization agreements for contact. One could argue that this interferes with the adoptive parents' rights and responsibilities as the legal and moral parents of the child. . . . Adoption was created out of the recognition that children need to feel secure about who their parents are and what their role is. If adoption professionals are candid, they will make sure that all people who place understand this completely before they consent to adoption.

Mary Beth Seader and William L. Pierce, in Debating Children's Lives. *Eds. Mary Ann Mason and Eileen Gambrill. Thousand Oaks: Sage Publications, 1994.*

Fearful of not being selected to adopt, Sue and Brad reluctantly met Lynn's unmarried expectant birth parents, Jill and Chris. Jill was a retail clerk and Chris was a college student. The foursome "clicked" and agreed with enthusiasm and relief to proceed with the adoption. Sue and Brad offered to provide letters and photographs. After Jill gave birth to Lynn, Sue proposed that visits with Lynn might ease Jill's considerable emotional pain at being unable to muster the emotional and financial resources needed to keep her baby. Sue and Brad presumed that only a few visits would be required to assist Jill, while Jill presumed that the door had been opened to ongoing contact.

From the time of Lynn's birth, with the help of their adoption agency, Sue, Brad, Jill, and Chris coordinated meeting times and places consistent with the four adults' schedules. Sue and Brad lived fifty miles away from the two different towns in which Jill and Chris lived. To make the visits, it was necessary for Sue to skip work and arrange after-school care for Sam. Sam was never included in the visits out of concern that seeing Lynn with her birth parents would deepen his sadness about the irretrievable loss of his own birth parents. Once when scheduling was a problem for Sue and Brad, an agency social worker offered to take Lynn to visit with Jill and Chris without them. Sue and Brad were distressed and insulted by the suggestion that they might permit someone outside the family and not a personal friend to take their daughter anywhere.

Visitation was a logistical problem that became an emotional problem as well. Initially, Sue did not much mind the visits. Brad, though enthusiastic about adoption, was not keen on the visits. He was often unavailable or uninterested in getting together with Jill and Chris. An "on again/off again" couple, the young birth parents were unhappy when Sue and Lynn visited them without Brad. They explained that because they had both grown up with uninvolved fathers, they experienced Brad's absences as rejection. Sue felt awkward getting together with Chris without Brad, because she felt sexually attracted to the good-looking father of her daughter.

Unanticipated Complexities

After the initial few visits, it seemed to the adoptive parents, Sue and Brad, that the birth parents' attention shifted away from their birth daughter Lynn, where they felt it should be. Jill, the birth mother, seemed to like to talk about herself and was kind but awkward handling Lynn. Jill clearly wanted more contact and connection among the group than the other three adults. For example, Jill wanted her stepsisters and an uncle in another state to meet Lynn. Jill wanted Brad and Sue to attend a musical event in another city in which Jill's best friend was performing. A college student still living at home with his mother, Chris had not expected post-adoption visits, only letters and photographs, as the four originally agreed. Chris was not especially attentive to Lynn. He fell asleep during one visit with Lynn and Sue. During another visit that Jill and Brad could not attend, Chris suggested that he, Sue, and Lynn go to a shopping mall. At the mall he made purchases, while Sue and Lynn, who by this time was a toddler, tagged along behind him.

Sue and Brad grew to feel that they were constructing a way of life that was unduly complex, confusing, and stressful. The lack of meaningful guidance or support from a changing array of agency social workers was discouraging. The adoptive parents' family and friends adored Lynn and Sam, but were suspicious of the birth parents. For their part, Sue and Brad came to doubt their abilities to raise Lynn competently, as one of four cooperating parents, each with issues and needs of his or her own. Sue and Brad had full-time professional careers, two adopted children, and large, close extended families that included aging parents, siblings, nieces, nephews, uncles, aunts, and cousins. Sue and Brad believed their family of four would be better if they limited contact with Chris and Jill to an exchange of letters and photographs a few times a year as originally agreed. There was no written agreement promising perpetual visitation. Sue and Brad met with their adoption agency to discuss discontinuation of face-to-face meetings before speaking to Jill and Chris. The agency advised them to do what they felt was best and what was most comfortable.

Perhaps not surprisingly, Jill, the birth mother, was upset by the decision to discontinue face-to-face visits. Neither Sue nor Brad felt that they had made promises. Jill felt that she had been misled by the agency, Sue, and Brad—perhaps intentionally. The four parents nonetheless planned and participated in a final face-to-face visit, shortly after Lynn's second birthday. Thereafter, using the adoption agency as an intermediary, Sue sent photographs and letters to Jill and Chris two or three times a year. Brad was uninvolved. After nearly three years of silence, Sue and Brad received separate letters from Jill and Chris expressing love for Lynn and a desire that periodic updates on her development continue.

A Moral Question

Was it wrong for Sue and Brad to pull back from open adoption? Did they violate their moral obligations to Jill and Chris? In general, does excluding birth parents merit moral condemnation? I would like to argue that, as a general matter, adoptive parents are not ethically bound to include birth parents in their lives. Instead, adoptive parents are bound to do what they can do well toward providing a good life for their children. The discharge of this obligation may or may not entail birth parent inclusion, depending upon individual circumstances. Of course, many adoptive parents will want to include birth parents significantly in their lives, and many will have good reasons to attempt even painful and inconvenient inclusion. For example, those who adopt older children with healthy ties to their birth families (and possibly foster families or others) are likely to have good reason to attempt to maintain those ties through some form of inclusion.

I . . . argue that adoptive families who prefer to end, limit, or forgo post-adoption contact with birth parents should not be subjected to automatic moral condemnation; instead, they should be supported in their good faith decisions by adoption professionals and policymakers. Birth parents and their families do not have a *prima facie* moral right to maintain contact with adopted kin, because such an ascription of right would be inconsistent with adoptive parents' *prima facie* rights and responsibilities as caretakers. I expect that critics of the traditional, nuclear, privatized, and exclusive family will balk at the direction of my argument. Yet even proponents of non-traditional, alternative models of the family and birth parent rights must recognize the importance to effective caretakers of secure spheres of agency, autonomy, and well-being.

As I hope to make clear, I do not think legislators should outlaw contact between birth and adoptive families, or even discourage it. However, I disagree with [the] perspective that open adoption is obligatory because the adoptive parents relationship with their children should be understood, by contrast to the biological parents' relationship with their children, as merely "a guardianship, a stewardship." Few practicing social workers explicitly portray adoptive parenting as mere "guardianship." But some social workers seem to believe that birth parents ought, in a moral sense, to have access to adopted children and adoptive families long after the judges' legal decrees are signed. They seem to urge thinking of adoption as enlarging the natural family to include birth parents and adoptive parents in a fused or blended family. But it remains plausible and morally legitimate to understand newborn adoption as configuring separate, new families altogether.

| "*[Adoptees] are the ones whose rights*
| *should be tantamount.*"

Adoption Records Should Be Unsealed

Lorraine Dusky

Adult adoptees should have legal access to their original birth certificates, argues Lorraine Dusky in the following viewpoint. Open records make it easier for adoptees to seek out their birth parents and learn about their heritage, a right that should not be denied to any adult, Dusky explains. Moreover, contrary to the claims of open-records critics, the majority of birth mothers do not wish to remain anonymous to their children. Most, in fact, have a strong desire to meet their offspring, she points out. Dusky is the New York state representative to the American Adoption Congress and the author of the memoir Birthmark.

As you read, consider the following questions:

1. Which states allow adult adoptees access to their original birth certificates, according to Dusky?

2. Which organizations have opposed open-records laws, according to the author?

3. What percentage of birth parents filed a "no contact" preference in Oregon in 2004, according to the author?

Lorraine Dusky, "Birth Mothers, Adoptees Have Right to Records," *Women's eNews*, December 29, 2004. Reproduced by permission.

On Monday, Janet Allen plans to walk into the Division of Vital Records Administration in Concord, N.H., and ask for a copy of her original birth certificate. It will be the first time she can legally obtain it.

Allen, 51, a state legislator, was adopted as an infant. In New Hampshire, where she was born and adopted, Allen has been denied the right to that singular piece of paper that contains the answer to one of life's most basic questions: Who am I? The change in the law occurs ... New Years Day, 2005. As one of the people who worked for the bill's passage, Allen will be first in line.

"I am no longer a child and am delighted to finally have the same rights as non-adopted adults," she says. "The law now guarantees that no one will ever again have to go before a judge to beg, plead and be humiliated for a piece of paper that belongs to him."

Why does it matter so much to her and thousands of other adopted people in the state? Because her original birth certificate—not the amended one she's had most of her life—contains the names of her birth parents, and thus the key to her identity and origin. With the names, adopted people can search out their natural parents and perhaps obtain not only answers, but also updated medical information as well as the possibility of an ongoing relationship.

Open-Records States

With the law's passage, New Hampshire will join six other states—Alabama, Alaska, Delaware, Kansas, Tennessee and Oregon—that allow individuals adopted as children the right to their original birth certificates.

Some states had open birth records until the 1960s and even into 1980s. But as adoption became more common following the sexual revolution of those times, most of the states left with open records closed them, sweeping aside the rights of adopted children, no matter their age, to investigate their origins.

The bills to modernize the laws encounter stiff opposition and intense lobbying in state legislatures everywhere from adoption agencies and attorneys, local Catholic charities, the Church of Jesus Christ of Latter-Day Saints, and state chapters of the American Civil Liberties Union.

Against these well-funded organizations, the impassioned pleas of adoptees asking for open records are nearly drowned out, even though they are the ones whose rights should be tantamount.

In numerous states, bills to open the records have either languished in committee or died at the end of a legislative session. The opposition always hinges on the supposed anonymity that the women who gave up their children 30, 40 years ago were promised then, and are said to fervently desire today.

Forced Anonymity

I am one of those women, and I was not "promised" anonymity from my daughter. It was forced on me like a pair of manacles. The relinquishment papers gave me no opportunity to confirm or deny whether I might want to know her one day. There were no boxes to check marked either "contact desired" or "no contact." The papers merely stated that I was turning over my daughter to the state. The document promised nothing, not even that she would be adopted.

Our forced anonymity is a by-product of laws that seal the original birth certificate from the adopted person, designed to give adoptive parents the feeling their adopted children are really "theirs." Love was expected to quell curiosity. We birth mothers were supposed to "get on with our lives."

I protested to my social worker because never to know my own child sounded like living death. But I felt I had no choice; I signed the papers.

How Many Adoptees Search?

Opponents to open records claim that only 2% of all adoptees want to search—a minority within a minority. Their estimate is probably correct. On a yearly basis it is estimated that between 2% and 4% of all adoptees search, but a different 2% every year. This means if 2%, or 250,000, different adoptees search each year, in 10 years the number would total 2,500,000. The tremendous growth in the number of search and support groups is further evidence that not only adoptees, but relatives and others touched by adoption, are increasingly interested in searching, so these estimates may be very conservative. And, one may also argue that 100% of adoptees search. It may not be a literal search, but it is a meaningful one none the less. It begins when the child first asks herself or others, why was I adopted?

Kate Burke, The Decree, *vol. 13, 1996.*

I am not alone. The vast majority of us desperately want to know our children. We pray for the knock on the door, the phone call that will begin our healing.

How many of us are there? Probably between 5 million and 6 million, given the best estimate of "stranger" adoptions, those in which the baby is not given to a family member. How many of us seek reunion? There is no accurate way to know. But data from Oregon, which has allowed adoptees access to their original birth certificates since 2000, is as good an indicator as any.

Few Check "No Contact"

As part of the new law, Oregon gave birth mothers, as well as fathers, a chance to file a "no contact" preference. Near the end of 2004, nearly 8,000 adoptees had requested and received their original birth certificates. Eighty-three birth parents had asked for no contact, just a smidgeon over 1 percent.

In New Hampshire, the group of adoptees and birth parents who fought for open records has sent an e-mail alert that has been bouncing around the Web for the last month [November 2004] trying to ferret out New Hampshire birth mothers, assuming most will want to update their names and addresses so their children can find them.

Of course, there will be some who ask for no contact.

I try to sympathize with those women who want to hide from their own children. Perhaps they never told their husbands or their other children. Perhaps they have buried the secret so deeply—because it hurts too much to do otherwise—that they can not even imagine dealing with a flesh-and-blood person who asks "why?" Perhaps they are too guilty to face the child, now grown.

Changing Attitudes

If you knew me when my daughter was born, in 1966 in Rochester, N.Y., you might guess I would be one of them today. The father, a married man with a public life, had to be "protected." For his sake, and yes, mine, I operated in deepest secrecy. A Catholic girl a year out of college, so deep was my shame that I hid my pregnancy from my family in another state.

But times and attitudes change. As far back as 1980, after holding numerous hearings around the country, the then Department of Health, Education and Welfare proposed a Model Adoption Act that would have opened the records.

"There can be no legally protected interest in keeping one's identity secret from one's biological offspring; parents and child are considered co-owners of the information regarding the event of birth," it stated. "The birth parents' interest in reputation is not alone deserving of constitutional protection." But while some provisions of the act became national policy, this did not.

I am no longer the terrified young thing I was back in 1966.

Years ago, I decided I couldn't wait for Congress, or New York's legislature, to act; I paid a searcher $1,200. Within weeks I had my daughter's name and phone number and made that scary phone call to her other mother. Our daughter was still a teen-ager. I met her and her family in a matter of days.

That was more than two decades ago.

At my daughter's wedding, I stood next to her other mother during the ceremony. Yes, I was the one who didn't know a lot of people there, but my brothers and their wives, and some of their kids, were there too. It was a happy event for everyone. It was as it should be.

| *"Reunions between adoptees and birth mothers are not always successful."*

Unsealing Adoption Records Could Have Negative Consequences

Mary Kenny

In England a recently implemented law allows birth parents and other blood relatives to easily trace their adopted relatives. Freelance writer Mary Kenny expresses reservations about this law in the following viewpoint. Originally, only adoptees themselves were given access to their records, Kenny explains. But a law allowing biological parents to seek out the children they relinquished could disrupt an adoptee's life, the author asserts. Some adoptive parents also feel concerned about how intrusive and destabilizing the sudden appearance of a birth parent could be, notes Kenny.

As you read, consider the following questions:

1. The new British law allows adoptees to refuse contact with biological parents. Why does Kenny see this as potentially burdensome for adoptees?

2. How has adoption evolved since World War II, according to the author?

3. What percentage of adopted children who had reunified with their birth mothers discontinued contact or were rejected by their birth mothers, according to Kenny?

The Adoption and Children Bill, to be implemented [in 2004], will make it easier for mothers whose children were adopted to trace their sons and daughters. All blood relatives will have the same right. Until now, the initiative in tracing has been left to adopted people. All this may seem eminently fair to biological—or birth—mothers, but what of the women who have adopted children, taken them into their families and brought them up as their own? How do they feel about the new arrangements?

'I feel a bit of a dinosaur about this,' says Vicky, the mother of two children in their teens, both adopted. 'I am a feminist; I read the *Guardian*: I am in favour of progressive measures, and I feel I should be wholeheartedly in favour of these new regulations, but . . . it worries me. It worries me for the sake of my children.

'I actually asked both of them what they would feel about their birth parents contacting them. My 17-year-old, who likes to act tough, shrugged and said, "Well, I suppose I wouldn't mind—maybe they'd give me some cash!" My 13-year-old, who is a sensitive type, said thoughtfully, "People might be longing to know what's happened to the children they've given birth to, but I wouldn't like anything to happen suddenly."' That rather expresses the fears of many adoptive mothers: the dreaded vision of a strange woman waiting outside the school gates and announcing herself as the children's 'real' mother. (There was an episode in the TV serial *Grange Hill* which portrayed a birth mother locating her child in this way.)

Marion's Story

Marion, whose adopted children are now in their thirties, feels more inclined to accept the proposed changes, partly because her daughter and son are now married and settled with families of their own, and partly because she and her husband adopted their first child through a 'third-party adoption' procedure. That is, Marion and her husband knew the birth mother and her family, although the adoption was arranged through the proper legal channels. That first child is 'quite interested' in being approached by his birth mother, though he has never made the move himself. The second child has no interest in establishing a link with her birth parents, though she would probably not rebuff it.

'I feel such admiration for these birth mothers, who gave up their children for adoption—they were so brave,' says Marion. 'I wouldn't wish to deny them the chance of finding out about their children. They may just want to be reassured that they are all right. Mine are, I think, old enough to handle these things now, but when they were growing up they didn't want to be labelled "adopted". They always knew they were adopted, but they just didn't want to be put into a category. When my husband's name was to appear in a reference book, they wanted to be listed as our children, not as "by adoption".' When Marion's husband was seriously ill, his adopted children were as devoted to him as any biological offspring could have been.

A Variety of Reactions

The reaction of the children themselves to the new regulations may depend on many things: on the age or the personality of the adopted child, and in some cases on the circumstances. A child who was adopted from an abusive family may not be best pleased to have a distressed or needy biological mother suddenly reappearing in his life. Other adopted children may be pleased; in well-known cases, such as that of Pauline Prescott and Clare Short, these reunions have been delightful. But according to Hazel, whose adopted children are in their twen-

Creating Trouble and Turmoil

Anecdotal evidence indicates that often opening old records meant to be closed creates trouble and turmoil. The mother may have a cherished civic reputation and a new family that does not know of her youthful indiscretion. There is unlikely to be any emotional or cultural bond between mother and child after all those years. In one notorious case, a black man who was the child of a rape knocked on the door of his middle-aged white birth mother and sent her into terrified shock.

Many adoptees say they simply wish to have more information and are not out to embarrass birth mothers. But with open records they can do both.

Marianne Means, Liberal Opinion Week, *June 19, 2000.*

ties, such reunions work best because the adopted person has sought out the birth mother, and the initiative should still be left with the adoptee.

Under the new regulations, the adoptee will have the right to refuse contact with biological relations, but, says Hazel, 'that is an emotional burden being put on them—they then have the responsibililty, and perhaps even the guilt, of having turned away their birth family'.

For the Sake of the Child

It is not, says Hazel, that adoptive mothers feel threatened on their own behalf; it is that they worry for the sake of the child. 'We are just as tigerish in defence of our children as any other mother.' Her eldest son likes life to be regular and ordered; he is the sort of person for whom stability and security are very important. She cannot imagine what the impact might be if he received a letter saying the birth mother seeks contact.

'If he wants to do it himself, that's fine. But how dare anybody intrude into the lives of my children, retrospectively?' Hazel may not feel threatened, but she is angry: she feels that the law should not be altered now. When she and her husband adopted, the notion that the birth mother could afterwards come looking for them was not in the contract.

But as Vicky points out, adoption has evolved over the decades since the second world war. Unmarried mothers in the 1940s and 1950s were virtually forced to put their babies up for adoption and were often deeply distressed by the experience. This social pressure continued into the 1960s, when it was, unsurprisingly, altered by the 1967 Abortion Act, which gave women with unwanted or accidental pregnancies the choice. Most subsequently chose abortion, others began to choose single parenting, and the adoption rate dropped almost overnight.

The mothers whose children were adopted in the 1970s and 1980s were more likely to have chosen the option freely, and to have been given support by family, charities or social services. In Vicky's case, the birth mothers of both her children were young unmarried girls who accidentally became pregnant but refused an abortion on grounds of conscience. It is probable that mothers who voluntarily choose adoption might be less likely to 'intrude', suddenly, in their biological children's lives than older women who had babies wrenched from their arms 40 or 50 years ago.

Adoptive Mothers' Concerns

Adoptive mothers feel there should be further consultation about this change before it is fully implemented. Research into reunions after adoption is continuing: a new study from the Children's Society indicates that reunions between adoptees and birth mothers are not always successful. Sixty per cent of adopted children who made contact with their birth mothers dropped the contact after making it—or were eventually rejected by their biological mother. Blood is not always thicker than water, and maternal feelings by adoption can be stronger than those forged by biological birth.

| "Some [biological] families cannot be 'fixed' no matter how many resources are expended."

Foster Care and Adoption Are Preferable to Family Preservation

Connie Marshner

Short-term foster care followed by adoption is the best solution for children who cannot live with their biological families, argues Connie Marshner in the following viewpoint. Child welfare workers, however, typically keep children in the foster care system or aim to reunify children with their families of origin. In Marshner's opinion, these efforts are counterproductive. Years of foster care have a negative effect on children, and the biological parents of foster children are often abusive, she points out. Rather than wasting resources on reforming and preserving biological families, policy makers should promote the adoption of foster children, she maintains. Marshner is director of the Center for Governance at the Free Congress Foundation.

As you read, consider the following questions:

1. According to the National Center for Health Statistics, how many married American women are currently seeking to adopt children?

Connie Marshner, "Reform the Nation's Foster Care System Now," www.frc.org, October 17, 2005. Reproduced by permission of Family Research Council, 801 G Street, NW, Washington, DC 20001.

2. What kind of abuse is a factor in most foster care cases, according to the author?

3. In Marshner's opinion, why do child welfare workers avoid adoption as an option for foster children?

T he problems in our country's foster care system are largely due to a lack of accurate information. Fundamental ignorance of facts becomes the basis for policy decisions that impact the lives of many children. Scholarly authors claim that the number of children in need of adoptive homes is increasing while the number of prospective adoptive parents is decreasing. A solution, they argue, would be to open the pool of prospective adoptive parents to gays and lesbians. This position ignores the facts. . . .

Numbers of Possible Adoptive Parents

Many in the helping professions advocate alternative family structures as a solution to the shortage of foster parents. A case in point is a recent article in *Social Work* journal. Provocatively titled "Gay and Lesbian Adoptive and Foster Care Placements: Can They Meet the Needs of Waiting Children?" its bias is evident from the beginning. The authors claim that the number of children in need of adoptive homes is increasing while the number of prospective adoptive parents is decreasing. They argue that one potential way of increasing the pool of adoptive parents is to increase placements with gay and lesbian persons.

Data on adoption seekers, however, shows that there are more married couples seeking to adopt than there are adoptable children in foster care. According to the National Center for Health Statistics, one out of four women who have been married has considered adoption (9.9 million). A total of 232,000 are currently seeking or planning to adopt and have taken steps to do so. Also, many married women are open to adopting older children. Nearly 60 percent of these women would prefer to adopt a child under age two, but 37 percent would accept a child older than twelve. A third said they would be willing to adopt a child with severe disabilities, while 83 percent would accept a mildly disabled child.

The *Social Work* argument is a red herring. The reason children remain in foster care is not because there are no pro-spective parents—it is because social workers do not want to get them out of the system. But more on that later.

Who Are the Children in Foster Care?

AFCARS [Adoption and Foster Care Analysis and Reporting System] data is limited (eleven states have never met AFCARS conformity standards), but it is, nonetheless, the best currently available about children in foster care. From it, we know a few demographic facts:

- Most of the children in foster care are not infants. Just over half are age 10 or under and only 4 percent are under age one. Twenty-eight percent are age 11–15, 16 percent are 16–18 years old and 2 percent are age 19 or older.

- Ninety percent of the children fell in one of three eth-nic categories: black non-Hispanic (39 percent), white non-Hispanic (34 percent), and Hispanic (17 percent).

- Although fully 28 percent were less than a year of age when they were removed from their parents (35,732), most were older, including 31 percent between the ages of six and 15.

Why Do Children Enter Foster Care?

According to the *2000 Green Book*, "Most children enter foster care as a result of child abuse or neglect. . . . Substance abuse is cited as a factor in many of the cases coming to the atten-tion of child welfare agencies. . . ." An HHS [Health and Hu-man Services] publication, *Child Welfare Outcomes 1999: An-*

nual Report, provides additional detail on the types of abuse suffered:

- Almost three-fifths of all victims (58.4 percent) suffered neglect.

- One-fifth (21.3 percent) suffered physical abuse.

- About one out of 10 (11.3 percent) were sexually abused.

- More than one-third (35.9 percent) were victims of other or additional types of maltreatment.

The major reason children enter foster care is that the federal Child Abuse Prevention and Treatment Act of 1974 mandates the reporting, investigation, and treatment of child maltreatment cases. Reporting of suspected child maltreatment has more than quadrupled since 1976. The proportion of allegations that are substantiated upon investigation, however, has declined during the same period. In 1976, 65 percent of child abuse or neglect reports were substantiated; in 1990, 39 percent were substantiated; by 1998, only 29 percent were verified.

Certain factors occur in a majority of cases: substance abuse—including use of crack cocaine, smoking cigarettes, and drinking alcohol while pregnant—is the most common one. According to a National Institute on Drug Abuse survey of women who gave birth during 1992–93, 5.5 percent used illegal drugs while pregnant, 20.4 percent had smoked cigarettes, and 18.8 percent drank alcohol. The U.S. Department of Health and Human Services found that substance abuse is a factor in one-third to two-thirds of cases, and is a factor in two-thirds of the cases among children in foster care. According to the data, the typical profile of a substance-abusing parent is African-American (especially for cocaine), unmarried, and a welfare recipient.

One might hope that early intervention with the children of substance-abusing parents would lead to swift adoption.

Unfortunately, statistics do not bear this out. Public agencies seem to be having poor results even with infants placed under their charge—children so young that there are many families interested in adopting them. A 1997 study showed that two-thirds of the drug-exposed and more than half of the non-drug-exposed babies were still in care at two years of age. . . .

How Do Children Leave Foster Care?

There are three basic ways out of foster care: a child can be reunited with his family, "age out" of the system, or be adopted. Reaching age 18 with no family to depend upon for guidance, advice, or material or emotional help, presents a grim prospect indeed—particularly since those to whom it generally happens have been deprived of similar help for years. Given that the families of origin tend to be abusive to begin with, reunion with the family is not necessarily the best option. Adoption, therefore, may be the best outcome for children in the system.

Aging Out

Dr. Edmund Mech, a social work professor at the University of Illinois at Urbana-Champaign, has tracked the outcomes of foster care children for decades. He is particularly concerned about adolescents who age out of foster care without having the permanent family membership which can be gained through adoption, and has advocated supervised independent living as an option for older children in foster care. Mech quotes the National Research Council's Panel on High Risk Youth: "Adolescents who pass through the child welfare system are at high-risk of educational failure, unemployment, emotional disturbance, and other negative outcomes. Studies show that adolescents released from foster care fare far worse than either low-income youths or a cross-section of the general adolescent population."

As another study put it: "substantial proportion of youth who exit foster or group care experience negative outcomes

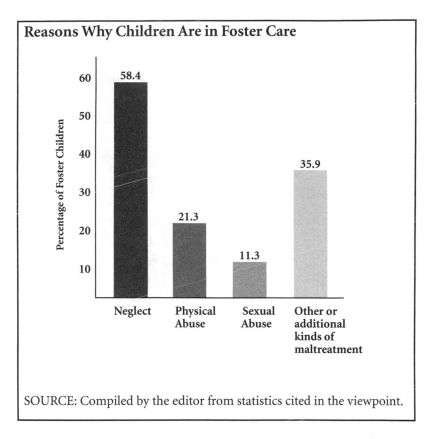

Reasons Why Children Are in Foster Care

Percentage of Foster Children

- Neglect: 58.4
- Physical Abuse: 21.3
- Sexual Abuse: 11.3
- Other or additional kinds of maltreatment: 35.9

SOURCE: Compiled by the editor from statistics cited in the viewpoint.

such as poor mental health or incarceration." Common sense and experience join the National Research Council in arguing that simply aging out of foster care, without a supervised and assisted transition into young adulthood, is an outcome not likely to succeed.

Family Reunification

Many children are reunited with their families under the child welfare policy of family preservation. Family preservation is a theory which was invented by judges and social workers, who saw it as a sort of penumbra emanating from the Adoption Assistance and Child Welfare Act of 1980. It is the notion that a child should be returned, at all costs, to the family of origin—even when that family is seriously abusive and parental rights could be legally terminated.

Towards that end, counseling, drug detoxification, employment services, and numerous other services—sometimes spanning years to deliver—are given to parents whose children have been taken into foster care, in the hope that the family will become sound enough to receive its children back again.

The problem with the theory is that it doesn't work. Some families cannot be "fixed" no matter how many resources are expended. In addition, years of foster care have a deleterious effect on children, who take emotional and behavioral problems back into the family when reunited. Children returned to partially-fixed families are likely to end up in the foster care system once again, older and more wounded.

Nonetheless, family preservationists hold that continuing to care for a child within the context of the family of origin should be the first priority. Dr. Richard Barth, arguably the best-known researcher looking at foster care, puts that option in its proper place when he says that "family continuity does not necessarily predict a successful transition to adulthood that is healthy for children or provides social benefits to the community.". . .

The Third Exit Route: Adoption

Since the other two routes fail to produce successful outcomes, it would be wonderful to be able to cite a popular and successful option. Unfortunately, however, very few foster care children are actually adopted. According to AFCARS, only 16 percent of the children exiting foster care in FY [fiscal year] 1999 (38,944) did so for the purpose of adoption.

Adoption is the best option for children who cannot live with their biological parents. "Adoption is a time honored and successful service for children and parents. The outcomes of adoption are more favorable for children than any social program I know," observes Dr. Richard Barth, a professor of social work at the University of North Carolina, and a leading expert on adoption.

Dr. Mech pronounced adoption a "proven option" more than 30 years ago, after reviewing 15 adoption follow-up studies conducted in the period 1924–1970. "Results obtained indicated that 75 percent, or nearly three in every four placements, were judged as successful," says Mech. Numerous studies, sponsored and published by entities as diverse as the Search Institute of Minneapolis and the *Journal of Marriage and the Family*, find that adopted children enjoy a quality of life substantially above and beyond that of their non-adopted counterparts.

Termination of the parental rights of the abusive or neglectful parents is the first legal step in the adoption process. While the data show that at the end of the FY 1999 there were 127,000 children in foster care waiting to be adopted (up from 122,000 in FY 1998), the data also show that only 64,000 children in foster care had their parental rights terminated for all living parents. Since the termination of parental rights (TPR) process is usually begun at the initiation of the caseworker, this much lower figure suggests social workers are in fact seriously considering adoption only for a relatively small number of foster care children. . . .

Obstacles to Adopting Foster Children

Why are not more children adopted?

At risk of being too blunt, it is worth quoting Mech, who summarizes the barrier to adoption in two sentences: "In seeking answers, child welfare experts avoid adoption as an alternative. Solutions proposed are primarily agency-based." Translated for policymakers, this means: If children are adopted, the involvement of the agencies and their staff ends; all the other solutions or options require more or less continuous involvement by social workers with the child and the family of origin or the foster caregivers. In short, avoiding adoption ensures full employment for social workers.

Of course, that is not stated so baldly. Rather, two main barriers appear in policy and practice: residual racism and the bias toward family preservation. Recent laws have been enacted to overcome these obstacles. However, the child welfare establishment, which opposed their enactment, now opposes their implementation as well. Good legislation has been stonewalled or eviscerated at the operational level.

"It's the people who want to abandon family preservation who have a lot of explaining to do."

Family Preservation Is Preferable to Foster Care and Adoption

National Coalition for Child Protection Reform

Many family policy experts promote foster care and adoption for children born into abusive or neglectful families. Believing that attempts to reform troubled families puts children at risk, these experts are against family preservation. In the following viewpoint the National Coalition for Child Protection Reform (NCCPR) argues that foster care can be more dangerous than a child's original family. In states that have rejected family preservation in favor of foster care, child abuse deaths of foster children have actually increased, the author notes. Reunifying biological families is preferable to letting children linger in overburdened foster care systems, the coalition concludes. The NCCPR is an organization that promotes child welfare reform.

As you read, consider the following questions:

1. What event started the Illinois foster care panic, according to the NCCPR?

2. According to the authors, what did Illinois officials do in the late 1990s when they ran out of places to house foster children?

National Coalition for Child Protection Reform, "Foster Care Panics," www.nccpr.org, August 12, 2005. Reproduced by permission.

3. Why were family preservation workers not able to save the life of Joseph Wallace, according to the NCCPR?

W e don't have to guess what will happen if opponents of family preservation get what they want. We don't have to guess what will happen if family preservation is effectively abandoned.

We don't have to guess, because it happened—in Illinois in 1993, in New York City in 1996 and in Florida in 1999.

In April 1993, three-year-old Joseph Wallace was killed by his mother. Joseph was "known to the system." "Family preservation" quickly became the scapegoat. It was attacked relentlessly by politicians and much of the media—even though most of the programs in Illinois bore little resemblance to the effective, Homebuilders-based models used in other states.[1]

As a result, workers and judges became terrified to leave or return any child home for fear of becoming the next target of politicians and the Chicago media. Almost all efforts to keep families together were effectively abandoned amid claims that such efforts contradict "child protection." Indeed, Illinois legislators added the words "best interests of the child" to their child welfare law in at least 30 different places to make sure everybody got the point.

The Illinois Foster Care Panic

By 1996, a child was more likely to be placed in foster care in Illinois than in any other state. But instead of saving lives, child abuse deaths went up. They soared from 78 before family preservation was abandoned to 82 the first year after, to 91 in fiscal 1997. That's not surprising. The abandonment of family preservation led to a foster care panic that overwhelmed the system to the point that it created a backlog of more than

---

1. Homebuilders interventions offer intensive counseling and training to troubled families, including assistance with financial problems and help with job training, day care, and practical skills.

5,000 uncompleted investigations. In the first two years of the panic, foster care placements in the Illinois foster care population soared by 44. Child abuse deaths *in* foster care in Illinois went from zero in the year before the foster care panic to five in the first year afterwards—an all-time record.

The pattern showed itself in a new way in fiscal 1998, when the Illinois foster care panic finally began to abate. That year, the number of child abuse deaths finally fell below the number before the panic began. *And that year also was the first year since the panic in which the total number of Illinois children in foster care actually declined.* The decline has continued; indeed, Illinois reversed course, embraced family preservation and cut its foster care population dramatically. And at the same time, safety outcomes have improved.

Other Child Welfare Tragedies

But during the years family preservation was abandoned, it led to other tragedies in Illinois:

- Having supposedly "put children first," Illinois officials soon found they had no place to put children at all. So they ware jammed into a hideous shelter, then overflowed into offices. Streetwise teens were thrown together with vulnerable younger children; infants were jammed into urine-soaked cribs. An 11-year-old got hold of a gun and fired it.

- Children were jammed into any foster home with a bed, with little screening of foster parents or foster children. As a result, according to Benjamin Wolf of the Illinois Affiliate of the American Civil Liberties Union, the Illinois foster care system became "like a laboratory experiment to *produce* the sexual abuse of children."

- A study by the Child Welfare Institute found that, as a result of the foster care panic, *at least* one third of the children now in foster care in Illinois could safely have been returned to their own homes.

Abandoning family preservation took a bad system and made it, in Wolf's words, "unquestionably worse."

Case History: In the Chicago Shelter

What was it like for children suddenly swept up in the Chicago Foster Care Panic, taken from their parents and left in the city's makeshift shelter? This account is from the *Chicago Tribune*:

> A surly teenager with a bad attitude struts and shouts swear words a few yards away from the abused and neglected little ones, so young they can barely tell you their names ... 16-year-old Harry is boasting: 'I stole 50 cars this week!' A few yards away is 5-year-old Michael, so very scared and trying with all his might not to cry. 'I'm the big brother,' Michael explains, gently stroking the hair of Christopher, 4, who gulps heavy, sleepy breaths and sucks his thumb on a cot in a corner. . . . When a visitor tried to shake the little boy's hand, he threw his arms around her, starving for a hug. . . . 'I want my mom,' Michael said . . .

And what about the case that started it all? What was the role of family preservation in the case of Joseph Wallace? A family preservation worker recommended that the Wallace family *not* be preserved—he recommended to a judge that the child be removed. The judge agreed. The child was removed, but the records were lost when the family moved to another county. Only then was the child sent home to his death.

Not only was family preservation not the cause of the Wallace death—family preservation almost saved Joseph Wallace's life.

Other Foster Care Panics

Nearly three years later it was New York City's turn. Again, this time in late 1995, a child "known to the system" died. Again officials blamed "family preservation"—even though

---

Facts About Family Preservation

- Most families, when properly assisted, can care for their children successfully.

- Children need to be with their families, and even in the most troubled families, separation is a traumatic event for both child and family.

- Within 24 hours of a referral to Family Preservation Services (FPS), a response is made to the family.

- Evaluation of FPS programs around the country report on average 80 percent of families that have received FPS remain together after one year.

Anne Herrick, "Information Packet: Family Preservation,"
National Resource Center for Foster Care and
Permanency Planning, 2002.

---

deaths of children previously known to the child welfare system had declined by more than 40 percent since 1991. Once again, they set off a foster care panic, overwhelming the system. The result: Thousands of children were forced to sleep, often on chairs and floors, in a violence-plagued, emergency makeshift shelter created from city offices, a four-year-old foster child was beaten and starved to death in a foster home opened by one private agency, apparently desperate for beds, after another had closed it down, and the decline in child abuse deaths ended. Between 1996 and 1998, deaths of children previously "known to the system" increased by 50 percent. Just as in Illinois, the death toll among children known to the system fell below the pre-panic level only after the panic had abated in 1999 and the City was taking away fewer children. Like Illinois, New York City learned from its mistakes, reversed course, and embraced family preservation.

And then came Florida. The death of a child "known to the system" and the appointment of a state child welfare agency chief staunchly opposed to keeping families together combined to set off a foster care panic in 1999. Again the foster care population soared. And again, deaths of children "known to the system" increased, from an average of 25 per year in the four years before the Florida Foster Care Panic to an average of 32 per year in the five years since.

These data don't prove that child abuse deaths always will go up when family preservation is abandoned. But the critics of family preservation premise their entire argument on the assumption that if family preservation is eliminated, or at least drastically curtailed, such deaths will decrease.

At a minimum, the results from Illinois, New York, and Florida—particularly when compared to states like Alabama, and to what happened when Illinois and New York reversed course—suggest that it's the people who want to abandon family preservation who have a lot of explaining to do. It's time for the burden of proof to shift from those who want to keep more children with their parents to those who want to take them away.

Periodical Bibliography

The following articles have been selected to supplement the diverse views presented in this chapter.

Janet Albrechtsen   "Restoring Adoption," *Quadrant*, January/February 2002.

Erwin A. Blackstone and Simon Hakim   "A Market Alternative to Child Adoption and Foster Care," *Cato Journal*, Winter 2003.

Devon Brooks, Sigrid James, and Richard P. Barth   "Preferred Characteristics of Children in Need of Adoption: Is There a Demand for Available Foster Children?" *Social Service Review*, December 2002.

Steve Christian   "Healing the Hole in the Heart," *State Legislatures*, December 2002.

Rachel Foggitt   "Unforgettable," *Community Care*, March 10, 2005.

Pam Harvey-Fulton   "My Mother the Stranger: When the Woman Who Gave Birth to Me Finally Came to Visit My Family, It Was Clear to Me We Share Nothing Besides Genes. Should I Feel Guilty?" *Toronto Globe and Mail*, December 9, 2004.

Alyssa Katz   "No More Excuses," *City Limits*, December 2003.

Lisa Rauschart   "Not 'Unadoptable': New Effort to Find Homes for Older Foster Children," *World & I*, August 2004.

Sarah Saffian   "I Finally Found My Birth Mother," *Cosmopolitan*, December 2002.

Peg Tyre   "Seek and You May Find," *Newsweek*, August 1, 2005.

Rosemary Zibart   "Teens Wanted: Adopt an Adolescent? Yes, There Are Families Crazy and Loving Enough to Take That On," *Time*, April 4, 2005.

For Further Discussion

Chapter 1

1. J.C. Willke contends that, on average, adopted children have less health, academic, and behavioral problems than do nonadopted children raised by single parents. Lori Carangelo disagrees, arguing that adopted children are at risk of developing behavioral problems and violent tendencies. What evidence do these authors use to support their conclusions? Which evidence is more convincing, in your opinion?

2. Adam Pertman maintains that some health counselors fail to provide women with unbiased information regarding their pregnancies. Do you believe that it is wrong to promote adoption over abortion or single motherhood? Why or why not? Use citations from the text in defending your answer.

3. After reading this chapter, would you be more likely to advise an unmarried woman with an unwanted pregnancy to keep her baby, to relinquish it for adoption, or to have an abortion? Explain.

Chapter 2

1. Gary Clapton discusses the conclusions he drew from his in-depth study of thirty men who had children who were given up for adoption. In your opinion, what are the drawbacks of a study involving such a small number of people? What are the benefits? Do you think that Clapton's findings prove that biological fathers need more representation in the adoption process? Why or why not?

2. This chapter examines the specific rights of birth mothers, birth fathers, adoptive parents, and adopted children. In your opinion, whose rights should be considered first? Whose rights should be considered last? Explain your answer.

Chapter 3

1. Arlene Istar Lev asserts that transracial adoption should be encouraged because there are many minority children who need permanent homes but not enough minority families to adopt them. The National Association of Black Social Workers maintains that promoting same-race adoptions is a more desirable solution to the disproportionate numbers of minority children in need of homes. After reading this chapter, which of these policies do you think adoption advocates should support? Cite passages from the text as you defend your answer.

2. Debbie Spivack is the executive director of an international adoption advocacy organization. Tobias Hubinette is ethnically Korean and was adopted by Swedish parents. How does this knowledge about their backgrounds affect your assessment of their contrasting arguments about international adoption? Explain.

3. Adam Pertman and the American Academy of Pediatrics maintain that children adopted by gays and lesbians fare as well as children raised by heterosexuals. Robert H. Knight contends that studies ostensibly proving the health of children raised by homosexuals rely on flawed data. Which argument do you find most convincing? Why?

Chapter 4

1. Brenda Romanchik believes that open adoption offers a way to create a unique blended family consisting of birth parents, adoptive parents, and adoptees. What reservations

does Anita L. Allen have about open adoptions? After reading these viewpoints, do you believe that open adoptions are preferable to closed adoptions? Explain.

2. After reading the viewpoints by Lorraine Dusky and Mary Kenny, whose rights do you think should receive more weight in the open-records controversy: the adoptee's, the birth mother's, or the adoptive family's? Why? Use citations from the text in defending your answer.

3. Connie Marshner and the National Coalition for Child Protection Reform have contrasting views on foster care and family preservation. What concerns do they share? On what specific points do they disagree?

Organizations to Contact

Abolish Adoption
PO Box 401, Palm Desert, CA 92261
e-mail: info@abolishadoption.com
Web site: www.abolishadoption.com

Abolish Adoption is an organization that petitions to end the practice of adoption. It believes that adoption is not in the child's best interests and that it violates human rights. Abolish Adoption also campaigns for open adoption records laws. Its publications include *The Ultimate Searchbook: Worldwide Adoption, Genealogy, and Other Search Secrets* by Lori Carangelo.

Adoption.com
800-ADOPT-HERE
Web site: http://adoption.com

Adoption.com is a Web-based network of adoption organizations. It features profiles of prospective adoptive parents and adoptable children, and it addresses adoption issues such as unintended pregnancy, international adoption, and adoption reunions. Several publications and magazines, such as *Adoptive Families* and *Adoption Today*, are available at this site.

Bastard Nation
PO Box 271672, Houston, TX 77277-1672
(415) 704-3166
Web site: www.bastards.org

Bastard Nation is an adoptee rights organization that campaigns to legalize adopted adults' access to records that pertain to their historical, genetic, and legal identity. It publishes the monthly newsletter *Byline*.

Child Welfare League of America (CWLA)
440 First St. NW, Third Floor, Washington, DC 20001-2085
(202) 638-2952 • fax: (202) 638-4004
Web site: www.cwla.org

CWLA, a social welfare organization, promotes the well-being of children, youth, and their families. A standards setter for welfare and human services agencies, CWLA encourages research on all aspects of adoption. It publishes the bimonthly *Child Welfare Journal* as well as *Children's Voice* magazine.

Concerned United Birthparents (CUB)
PO Box 503575, San Diego, CA 92150-3475 • (800) 822-2777
e-mail: info@CUBirthparents.org
Web site: www.cubirthparents.org

CUB provides assistance to birth parents, works to open adoption records, and seeks to develop alternatives to the current adoption system. It helps women considering the placement of a child for adoption make an informed choice and seeks to prevent unnecessary separation of families by adoption. CUB publishes the quarterly *CUB Communicator*.

Families Adopting Children Everywhere (FACE)
PO Box 28058, Baltimore, MD 21239
(410) 488-2656
e-mail: info@faceadoptioninfo.org
Web site: www.faceadoptioninfo.org

FACE provides support to adoptive parents and families and promotes legislation advocating children's rights. It also offers a class, "Family Building Through Adoption," through its Web site.

National Adoption Information Clearinghouse (NAIC)
Children's Bureau, Administration on Children, Youth, and
  Families 370 L'Enfant Promenade SW, Washington, DC
  20447
(703) 352-3488 • fax: (703) 385-3206

e-mail: naic@caliber.com
Web site: http://naic.acf.hhs.gov

A service of the Children's Bureau, Administration on Children, Youth, and Families, an arm of the U.S. Department of Health and Human Services, NAIC distributes publications on all aspects of adoption, including infant and international adoption, the adoption of special-needs children, and pertinent state and federal laws. For research, it provides an online database containing titles and abstracts of books, articles, and program reports on adoption.

National Coalition for Child Protection Reform (NCCPR)
53 Skyhill Rd., Suite 202, Alexandria, VA 22314
(703) 212-2006
e-mail: info@nccpr.org
Web site: www.nccpr.org

The members of the NCCPR have encountered the child welfare system in their professional capacities. It works to improve this system by changing policies concerning child abuse, foster care, and family preservation. Its publications include issue papers such as "Family Preservation and Adoption" and "Just Say No to the Orphanage."

National Council for Adoption (NCFA)
225 N. Washington St., Alexandria, VA 22314-2561
(703) 299-6633 • fax: (703) 299-6004
e-mail: www.ncfa-usa.org
Web site: www.ncfa-usa.org

Representing volunteer agencies, adoptive parents, adoptees, and birth parents, NCFA is devoted to serving the best interests of children through adoption. It strives for adoption regulations that will ensure the protection of birth parents, children, and adoptive parents. Its quarterly newsletter, the *National Adoption Report,* provides updates on state and federal legislative and regulatory changes affecting adoption. NCFA also publishes *Adoption Advocate* and *Adoption Factbook III.*

Resolve
7910 Woodmart Ave., Suite 1350, Bethesda, MD 20814
(301) 652-8585 • fax: (301) 652-9375
e-mail: info@resolve.org
Web site: www.resolve.org

Resolve is a nationwide information network serving the needs of men and women dealing with infertility and adoption issues. It publishes several fact sheets as well as the quarterly journal *Family Building* and the book *Resolving Infertility*.

Bibliography of Books

Joanne Baer — *Growing Up in the Dark: Adoption Secrecy*. Philadelphia: Xlibris, 2004.

Fiona Bowie, ed. — *Cross-Cultural Approaches to Adoption*. New York: Routledge, 2004.

David M. Brodzinsky and Jesus Palacios, eds. — *Psychological Issues in Adoption: Research and Practice*. Westport, CT: Praeger, 2005.

Nicky Campbell — *Blue-Eyed Son: The Story of an Adoption*. London: Pan Books, 2005.

E. Wayne Carp — *Adoption Politics: Bastard Nation and Ballot Initiative 58*. Lawrence: University Press of Kansas, 2004.

Gary Clapton — *Birth Fathers and Their Adoption Experiences*. Philadelphia: Jessica Kingsley, 2003.

Sue Elliott — *Love Child: A Memoir of Adoption and Reunion, Loss and Love*. London: Vermilion, 2005.

Karen J. Foli and John R. Thompson — *The Post-Adoption Blues: Overcoming the Unforeseen Challenges of Adoption*. New York: Rodale Books, 2004.

Laura Beauvais Godwin and Raymond Godwin — *The Complete Adoption Book: Everything You Need to Know to Adopt a Child*. Avon, MA: Adams Media, 2005.

Deborah D. Gray — *Attaching in Adoption: Practical Tools for Today's Parents*. Indianapolis: Perspectives Press, 2002.

James L. Gritter   *Lifegivers: Framing the Birthparent Experience in Open Adoption.* Washington, DC: Child Welfare League of America, 2000.

Sally Haslanger and Charlotte Witt, eds.   *Adoption Matters: Philosophical and Feminist Essays.* Ithaca, NY: Cornell University Press, 2005.

David M. Haugen   *Social Issues Firsthand: Adoption.* San Diego: Greenhaven Press, 2005.

Alice Hearst   *Crossing Cultures: Children, Identity, and the Politics of Interracial Adoption.* New York: Routledge, 2005.

Gregory C. Keck and Regina Kupecky   *Parenting the Hurt Child: Helping Adoptive Families Heal and Grow.* Colorado Springs, CO: Pinon Press, 2002.

Randall Kennedy   *Interracial Intimacies: Sex, Marriage, Identity, and Adoption.* New York: Pantheon, 2003.

Karen Salyer McElmurray   *Surrendered Child: A Birth Mother's Journey.* Athens: University of Georgia Press, 2004.

Barbara Melosh   *Strangers and Kin: The American Way of Adoption.* Cambridge, MA: Harvard University Press, 2002.

Stephen O'Connor   *The Orphan Trains: The Story of Charles Loring Brace and the Children He Saved and Failed.* Boston: Houghton Mifflin, 2001.

Tim O'Hanlon and Rita Laws — *Adoption Digest: Stories of Joy, Loss, and the Journey.* Westport, CT: Bergin & Garvey, 2001.

Sandra Patton — *BirthMarks: Transracial Adoption in Contemporary America.* New York: New York University Press, 2000.

Joyce Maguire Pavao — *The Family of Adoption.* Boston: Beacon Press, 2005.

Adam Pertman — *Adoption Nation: How the Adoption Revolution Is Transforming America.* New York: BasicBooks, 2000.

Carol S. Prentice — *An Adopted Child Looks at Adoption.* Whitefish, MT: Kessinger, 2005.

Evelyn Burns Robinson — *Adoption and Recovery: Solving the Mystery of Reunion.* Christies Beach, South Australia: Clova, 2004.

Barbara Katz Rothman — *Weaving a Family: Untangling Race and Adoption.* Boston: Beacon Press, 2006.

Jayne E. Schooler and Betsie L. Norris — *Journeys After Adoption: Understanding Lifelong Issues.* Westport, CT: Bergin & Garvey, 2002.

Rita J. Simon and Rhonda M. Roorda — *Adoption Across Borders: Serving the Children in Transracial and Intercountry Adoptions.* Lanham, MD: Rowman & Littlefield, 2000.

Joanne Wolf Small — *The Adoption Mystique.* Bloomington, IN: Authorhouse, 2004.

John Triseliotis et al.	*Adopted People, Their Birth Mothers, and Adopted Parents: The Triadic Experience of Adoption.* Sussex, England: Gardners Books, 2005.
Jane Waters	*Arms Wide Open: An Insight into Open Adoption.* Bloomington, IN: Authorbooks, 2005.

Index

abandonment issues, 50

abduction, 69

Abolish Adoption, 211

abortion
    adoption should be promoted over, 34–37
    adoption should not be promoted over, 38–42
    open-records movement and, 165

Act to Provide for the Adoption of Children, 15

Adopted Child Syndrome (ACS), 26–33

adoptees
    abandonment issues for, 50
    access to birth records for, 164–65, 180–85
        negative consequences of, 186–91
    benefits experienced by, 22–23, 43–47, 83
    closed adoption process and, 16
    from institutions, 45–46
    loss felt by, 19, 30
    psychological problems of, 19
    reunions between birth mothers and, 190–91
    rights of, should be protected, 82–88

adoption
    as best option, 19, 20, 44–47, 83–84
    can be harmful, 26–33
    closed, 15–16, 42, 164, 173
    encouragement of, 84
    far-reaching effects of, 53–54
    gay and lesbian, 91–92
        should be permitted, 131–38
        should not be permitted, 139–46

history of, 14–16

hostility toward, 117–18

is beneficial, 21–25

is preferable to family preservation, 192–200

is not preferable to family preservation, 201–6

negative consequences of, 19

privacy issues of, 87–88

should be promoted over abortion, 34–37

should not be promoted over abortion, 38–42

single mothers should choose, 43–47

single mothers should not necessarily choose, 48–54

transracial, 85
    should be encouraged, 93–101
    should not be encouraged, 102–12

violence and, 31–33

wrong reasons for choosing, 50–52

see also open adoption

Adoption and Children Bill, 187

Adoption and Safe Families Act (ASFA), 104

Adoption Assistance and Child Welfare Act, 197

Adoption.com, 211

adoption fees, 118–19

adoption placements
    in mother-father households, 85–86
    in single-parent households, 86–87

adoption process
    protection of rights in, 57–58
    of adopted children, 82–88
    of adoptive parents, 78–81

of birth father, 70–77
of birth mother, 59–69
adoption professionals
   attitudes of, toward birth
      parents, 75–77
   coercion by, of birth mother,
      59–69
   should be culturally aware,
      109
adoption records
   opening of sealed
      debate over, 164–65
      is adoptee's right, 180–85
      negative consequences of,
         186–91
   sealed, in closed adoptions,
      15
adoptive parents
   are real parents, 84–85
   concerns of, about open
      records, 186–91
   custody battles between birth
      parents and, 57
   hopes of, 50–52
   lack of connection between
      birth parents and, 15–16
   numbers of possible, 193–94
   relationship between birth
      parents and, in open adop-
      tions, 167–71, 174–79
   rights of, should be pro-
      tected, 78–81
African American children
   in foster care, 103–4, 106–7
   see also transracial adoption
African American families
   are available for adoptees,
      108
   need equal access to adop-
      tion, 111
   should be preserved, 102–12
Allen, Anita L., 172
Allen, Janet, 181
American Academy of Pediatrics
   (AAP), 92, 131, 142

American Psychological Associa-
   tion (APA), 91, 135
Annie H., 34
Arnold, Laurence, 31
attachment disorders, 28
Attention Deficit Disorder
   (ADD), 29

Babylonian Code of Hammurabi,
   14
Barth, Richard, 198–99
Bartholet, Elizabeth, 84
Bashir, Samiya, 108
Basore, Shannon, 52
Bastard Nation, 211
Being Adopted (Brodzinsky et al.),
   30
Benedict XVI (pope), 156
biological father. *See* birth father
biological mother. *See* birth
   mother
biological parents. *See* birth parents
birth father
   consent by, 57
   experiences of, 71, 73
   negative views of, 75–77
   proof of fatherhood by,
      74–75
   rights of, 57–58
      should be protected, 70–77
birth mother
   benefits of adoption for,
      23–25
   closed adoption process and,
      15–16, 63–65
   connection between newborn
      and, 19, 30, 106
   consent by, 57
   emotional pain experienced
      by, 36–37
   forced anonymity for, 182–83
   lack of access to baby by,
      63–65

loss felt by, 51
love felt by, for child, 53
privacy rights of, 164–65
reunions between children
  and, 190–91
rights of, should be protected,
  59–69
society's views of, 52–53
see also unwed mothers
birth parents
  closed adoption process and,
    15–16
  loss felt by, 51
  open adoptions and, 16–17,
    167–71, 173–79
  regrets experienced by, 49–54
  sealed records about, 15–16
  society's views of, 52–53
birth records
  access to, 164–65
    is adoptee's right, 180–85
    negative consequences of,
      186–91
  sealed, 15
Black Pulse Survey, 108
Blanc, Peter, 58
blended families, open adoptions
  as, 169–71
"body part/organ" rumor, 117
bonding, 106
Brodzinsky, David M., 30
Brown, Louise, 155
Burks, Kate, 183
Bush, George W., 154, 157, 158,
  159

Caesar, Julius, 14
Callahan, Patrick J., 32
Cameron, Paul, 92, 142
Campbell, Patrick, 31
Caplan, Arthur, 151
Carangelo, Lori, 26
Castelluci, Denise K., 165

Catholic Church
  on embryo adoption, 160
  on in vitro fertlization (IVF),
    156–57
child abuse
  in foster care, 202–6
  as reason for child removal,
    194–96
Child Abuse Prevention and Treatment Act, 195
child removals
  from African American fami-
    lies, 103–106
  reasons for, 194–97
  reunification efforts after, 110
children of color. *See* African
  American children; transracial
  adoption
child trafficking, 119–20
child welfare agencies
  obstacles to adoption by, 199–
    200
  should be monitored, 109–10
  treatment of African Ameri-
    cans by, 105–106
Child Welfare League of American
  (CWLA), 212
Christian Medical Association
  (CMA), 151
Clapton, Gary, 70
closed adoptions, 15–16, 164
  advocates of, 173
  promoted by NCFA, 42
cocaine exposure, 46
coercion tactics, 60–69
Columbia, 127
Concerned United Birthparents
  (CUB), 212
concurrent planning, 112
Cooke, David, 28
coparents
  legal status for, 136–37
  see also second-parent adop-
    tion

crimes, by adoptees against adoptive parents, 22, 31–33
cultural heritage, importance of, 99–100, 107
culture of life, 157–58, 160–61
custody battles, 57, 79–81

Dailard, Cynthia, 38, 41
DeBoer, Jessica, 79
de-colonization, 123–25
DeGellecke, Patrick, 31
Dershowitz, Alan, 27
Dobson, James, 156
Dorner, Patricia Martinez, 16, 169
drug exposure, in utero, 46
Dusky, Lorraine, 180

East Asia, 125
embryo adoption
    is hypocritical, 153–61
    should be encouraged, 147–52
England, 14–15
Ennis, Michael, 153
Ethiopia, 124, 127

families
    African American, 102–12
    efforts to preserve biological, 19
    nontraditional, 91–92
Families Adopting Children Everywhere (FACE), 212
Family in America, 43
family preservation, 49–50, 105
    foster care and adoption is preferable to, 192–200
    foster care and adoption is not preferable to, 201–6
Family Preservation Services (FPS), 205
Family Research Council, 159–60

family reunification, 197–98
Florida
    adoption law in, 57–58
    foster care system in, 206
    gay and lesbian adoption in, 134, 143
foreign adoption. *see* international adoption
foster care
    developmental issues affected by, 106–7
    is preferable to family preservation, 192–200
    is not preferable to family preservation, 201–6
    problems with, 110
    reasons for entering, 194–96, 197
    tragedies, 202–6
    ways of leaving, 196–99
        adoption, 198–99
        aging out, 196–97
        family reunification, 197–98
foster children, 44, 83
    African American, 103–4, 106–7
    need married parents, 140–42
    obstacles to adopting, 199–200
    statistics on, 194
foster parents, shortage of, 193
Frist, Bill, 154

gay and lesbian adoption, 91–92
    should be permitted, 131–38
    should not be permitted, 139–46
    of transracial children, 93–101
gay parenting studies, 142–44
Gladwell, Malcolm, 115
Golombok, Susan, 144

Gritter, Jim, 52
Grotevant, Harold D., 173

Harkin, Tom, 149
health care providers, training for, by NCFA, 39–42
Heikkila, Matthew, 31, 32
Henig, Robin Marantz, 30
HIV/AIDS, 145
Hollinger, Joan, 91
Holocaust, 123–24
homosexual adoption. *See* gay and lesbian adoption
homosexuality, health risks of, 144–45
homosexual parents
    children of, 135, 142–46
    parenting skills of, 91–92
    risk of death of, 142
homosexuals, life expectancy of, 142
Hopkins, Amanda, 79, 80–81
Hubinette, Tobias, 122
human embryos. *See* embryo adoption
Humphrey, Donald, 31

identity development, 106–107, 135
illegitimate children, 15
Illinois, foster care system in, 202–4
India, 124
Indian Child Welfare Act, 112
Infant Adoption Awareness Act (IAAA), 39
infants, bonds between mothers and, 19, 30, 106
inheritance laws, 14
institutionalized children, 45–46, 116
Interethnic Placement Act (IEPA), 104, 107–8

international adoption, 79, 85
    adoption fees in, 118–19
    vs. child trafficking, 119–20
    hostility toward, 117–18
    is harmful, 122–30
    outcomes from, 128–30
    public perceptions about, 120–21
    should be supported, 113–21
    social problems created by, 125–26
in vitro fertilization (IVF), 148, 151, 155–56
    see also embryo adoption

Jacoby, Jeff, 78
Jefferson, Thomas, 15
John Paul II (pope), 156–57
Johnson, Dana E., 44
Johnson, Kate, 149

Kahn, Jeffrey P., 157
Kaplan-Roszia, Sharon, 171
Kenny, Mary, 186
Kindertransport, 123
kinship care, 110–11
    see also family preservation
Kirschner, David, 28, 29, 31
Knight, Robert H., 139
Kodjo, Cheryl, 19–20
Korea, 125–26, 127
Korean War, 124

Lamda Legal Defense and Education Fund, 91
legal status, of coparents, 136–37
legitimation process, 14
Lerner, Robert, 143
lesbian adoption. *See* gay and lesbian adoption
Lev, Arlene Istar, 93
Lifton, Betty Jean, 31

love, for child, by birth mother, 53

Lowe, Heather, 48, 64

Lynn, Evelyn, 58

married parents, 85–86, 140–42

Marshner, Connie, 192

Maynard, Jennifer, 53

McRoy, Ruth G., 173

Means, Marianne, 165, 189

Mech, Edmund, 196, 199

mediated open adoptions, 173–74

mediation services, 111

Melina, Lois, 171

Melosh, Barbara, 14

Minnesota, 15

Moore, Mary Tyler, 149

mother-and-father parenting, 85–86

mother-love, 53

Multiethnic Placement Act (MEPA), 98, 104, 107–8

murder, of adoptive parents, by adoptees, 31–33

Murray, Suzanne, 149

Nagai, Althea, 143

National Adoption Information Clearinghouse (NAIC), 212–13

National Association of Black Social Workers (NABSW), 102

National Coalition for Child Protection Reform, 201, 213

National Council for Adoption (NCFA), 20, 39–42, 82, 213

National Embryo Donation Center, 152

newborns, loss felt by, 19, 30, 106

newspaper notices, 57–58

New York, foster care system in, 205

Nightlight Christian Adoptions, 158

nondirective counseling, 39–42

nontraditional families, 91–92

Olasky, Marvin, 45

open adoption
    debate over, 16–17
    defined, 167
    is not always feasible, 172–79
    mediated, 173–74
    privacy issues and, 87–88
    problems with, 175
    should be supported, 166–71
    time-limited, 173–74

open-records movement, 164–65

Origins Canada, 59

orphanages, 45–46, 116

orphans, 15

out-of-home placements
    dangers of, 106–7
    see also foster care

out-of-wedlock births, 22

paleo-psychological regression, 32

parental rights, termination of, 108–109, 199

parents. *See* adoptive parents; birth parents; foster parents

Parker, Su, 53

Paton, Jean, 27–28, 29

Patterson, Charlotte, 143

Pence, Mike, 148

Pertman, Adam, 38, 131

Pierce, William L., 175

Poor Law, 15

post-adoption services, 74

pregnancy counselors
    advice given to pregnant women by, 39–42
    coercion by, of birth mother, 59–69

pregnant teenagers
  benefits of adoption for, 24–25
  see also birth mother
Prescott, Pauline, 188
primal wound, 19, 30
primogeniture, 14, 15
privacy issues, 87–88
psychological problems
  Adopted Child Syndrome (ACS), 26–33
  caused by adoption, 19

racism
  in international adoption, 123, 127–28
  transracial adoption and, 94, 97, 99–100
Ratzinger, Joseph, 156
Reeve, Christopher, 149
religious organizations, on in vitro fertilization (IVF), 156–57
Resolve, 214
Romanchik, Brenda, 166
Rudd, Gene, 151–52

same-race adoption
  should be encouraged, 102–12
  see also transracial adoption
same-sex households, 91–92, 142–46
  see also gay and lesbian adoption
Santorum, Rick, 148
Schechter, Marshall D., 30
Schooler, Jayne E., 51
Schoor, Nanette, 19
Scott, Evan Parker, 79–81
Seader, Mary Beth, 175
Search Institute study, 22–23
secondary infertility, 54
second-parent adoption, 91, 133–34, 136–37

semi-open adoptions, 16, 167
serial killers, 32–33
sexual identity development, 135
sexually transmitted diseases, 145
Shawyer, Joss, 19
Shinto religion, 14
Short, Clare, 188
Silber, Kathleen, 16
single-parent adoption, 86–87
single-parenting
  vs. adoption, 45
  negatives of, 140–42
slave psychology, 28
Snowflakes program, 158–59
Sorosky, Arthur, 31
Spivack, Debbie, 113
stem cell research, 149–50, 154, 158, 159
Stem Cell Research Enhancement Act, 148
Stoddart, Ronald, 151
substance abuse, as reason for child removal, 104, 194–96
suicide rates, among international adoptees, 130
Swartz, Larry, 31–32
Sweden, 125–26, 127–28

Tankleff, Marty, 32
Tasker, Fiona, 144
Tate, Jeanne, 57–58
Tesdall, Sharon, 150
Thailand, 125
time-limited adoptions, 173–74
Tipping Point, The (Gladwell), 115
Tomassoni, Kathryn, 31
Tomassoni, Tammy, 31
torture, 27
transracial adoption, 85
  should be encouraged, 93–101
  should not be encouraged, 102–12

United States, adoption reform in, 15–16

Universal Declaration of Human Rights, 68–69

unwed mothers
benefits of adoption for, 23–25
nondirective counseling of, 39–42
removal of stigma on, 22
should choose adoption, 43–47
should not necessarily choose adoption, 48–54

stigmatized, 15, 164
see also birth mother

Verrier, Nancy, 19, 30
Vest, Cara, 152
Vietnam, 125
violence, adoption and, 31–33

Wallace, Joseph, 202, 204
Warburton, Danny, 79
White, Stephen, Jr., 80
Willke, J.C., 21
Wolf, Benjamin, 203
Wolff, Jana, 99